"*Self Analysis* teaches you that you can feel good. It is the positive lift for the human spirit."

Martha Pomroy, Attorney and Author

"It gave me a better understanding and awareness of what I was doing in my life."

Geoffrey Lewis, Actor

"One of the great things that *Self Analysis* did was improve my memory . . . it was so dramatic, that even my friends and family noticed."

Arlene Sue Farber, TV Producer

"*Self Analysis* opened a door of wonderful perceptions that I forgot I had."

Mickey McMeel, Actor and Musician

"My appreciation for art and life in general was increased enormously as a result of *Self Analysis*."

John E. Lux, Stock Broker

"A book of immense and immediate practical value, *Self Analysis* is as important as anything you will ever read."

Trevor Meldal-Johnsen, Author

"It's impossible to describe how much this book has changed my life. This is powerful data for those who dare to change."

Tamara Wilcox, Writer and Director

"This book is an essential first step for artists of all disciplines that wrongly believe any neurosis is essential to their creativity."

Dennis Dubin, TV Producer and Associate

L. RON HUBBARD

Self Analysis

"I like to help others and count it as my greatest pleasure in life to see a person free himself of the shadows that darken his days.

"These shadows look so thick to him, and weigh him down so, that when he finds they are shadows and that he can see through them and walk through them and be in the sun again, he is enormously delighted. And I am afraid I am just as delighted as he is."

L. RON HUBBARD

Self Analysis

A Simple Self-Help Volume of Tests and Techniques
Based on the Discoveries Contained in Dianetics

Publications International ApS

A **HUBBARD**® PUBLICATION

Published by
NEW ERA® Publications International ApS
Store Kongensgade 53
1264 Copenhagen K, Denmark

Printed in Denmark by
NEW ERA Publications International ApS

Hardback: ISBN 87-7336-191-7
Trade Paperback: ISBN 87-7336-193-3

To those hundreds of thousands of ardent[1]
Dianetics[2] *supporters who have carried the guidon*[3]
of sanity against the crumbling citadels[4]
of superstition and who have succeeded in rallying
to their standard[5] *the hopes of man.*

---

1.   ardent: full of ardor (great warmth of feeling), enthusiastic.
2.   Dianetics: Dianetics spiritual healing technology. The word is from the Greek, dia, "through,"
      and nous, "soul." It is a very exact analytical approach to the mind.
3.   guidon: a small flag or pennant used as a military unit's standard.
4.   citadel: a fortress overlooking a city.
5.   standard: 7. a distinctive flag.

Contents

Preface 1

Introduction 3

  I.   On Getting to Know Ourselves 9

  II.   On the Laws of Survival and Abundance 13

  III.   On the Death of Consciousness 17

  IV.   On Our Efforts for Immortality 21

  V.   On Raising Our Level of Consciousness 29

  VI.   On Raising Our Level of Life and Behavior 33

  VII.   The Hubbard Chart of Human Evaluation 41

  VIII.   Tone Scale[1] Tests 55

  IX.   How to Use the Disc 59

  X.   Processing[2] Section 63

       List 1: General Incidents 73

       List 2: Time Orientation 77

       List 3: Orientation of Senses 83

             Time Sense 83

             Sight 85

             Relative Sizes 87

             Sound 90

             Olfactory[3] 94

             Touch 99

             Personal Emotion 104

---

1.   tone scale: a scale that measures the emotional level of a person from apathy to enthusiasm and his survival potential.
2.   processing: the principle of making an individual look at his own existence, and improve his ability to confront what he is and where he is.
3.   olfactory: 1. of or pertaining to the sense of smell.

	Organic Sensation	119
	Motion Personal	122
	Motion External	125
	Body Position	128
List 4:	Standard Processing	131
List 5:	Assists to Remembering	139
List 6:	Forgetter Section	143
List 7:	Survival Factors	151
List 8:	Imagination	193
List 9:	Valences[4]	195
List 10:	Interruptions	201
List 11:	Invalidation	207
List 12:	The Elements	211
	Special Session Lists	215
	About the Author	221
	Glossary	225
	Index	235
	Bibliography	243
	Address List	251

---

4. valence: by a valence is meant an actual or a shadow personality. One's own valence is his actual personality.

Important Note

One of the biggest barriers to learning a new subject is its nomenclature, meaning the set of terms used to describe the things it deals with. A subject must have accurate labels which have exact meanings before it can be understood and communicated.

If I were to describe parts of the body as "thingamabobs" and "whatsernames," we would all be in a confusion, so the accurate naming of something is a very important part of any field.

A student comes along and starts to study something and has a terrible time of it. Why? Because he or she not only has a lot of new principles and methods to learn, but a whole new language as well. Unless the student understands this, unless he or she realizes that one has to "know the words before one can sing the tune," he or she is not going to get very far in any field of study or endeavor.[1]

Now I am going to give you an important datum:

The only reason a person gives up a study or becomes confused or unable to learn is because he or she has gone past a word that was not understood.

The confusion or inability to grasp or learn comes **after** a word that the person did not have defined and understood.

Have you ever had the experience of coming to the end of a page and realizing you didn't know what you had read? Well, somewhere earlier on that page you went past a word that you had no definition for.

Here's an example. "It was found that when the crepuscule arrived the children were quieter and when it was not present, they were much livelier." You see what happens. You think you don't understand the whole idea, but the inability to understand came entirely from the one word you could not define, *crepuscule*, which means twilight or darkness.

This datum about not going past an undefined word is the most important fact in the whole subject of study. Every subject you have taken up and abandoned had its words which you failed to get defined.

Therefore, in studying Self Analysis and Dianetics be very, very certain you never go past a word you do not fully understand. If the material becomes confusing or you can't seem to grasp it, there will be a word just earlier that you have not understood. Don't go any further, but go back to **before** you got into trouble, find the misunderstood word and get it defined.

L. Ron Hubbard

---

1.   endeavor: an earnest attempt or effort.

Footnotes and Glossary

The following glossary and footnote system has been employed to make it easy for the reader of this text to define words as he goes along, and thus prevent to a large degree any effects of misunderstood words that might otherwise occur.

The more difficult, unusual or technical words in this text are defined in footnotes at the bottom of the page the *first* time they appear in the text.

The words footnoted throughout the text and their definitions have been combined to form the Glossary at the end of the book. The number of the page where the word originally appeared is also noted.

The dictionaries that have been quoted for English word definitions are listed in the Glossary.

The footnotes are numbered and have a corresponding number where they appear in the text. In many cases there is a second number in front of the definition given. This is the number of the definition in the dictionary and indicates that there are more definitions in the dictionary than the one that is listed.

Words of Dianetics that are footnoted have definitions developed by the author in his researches.

New Words

In the search that brought about Dianetics many new phenomena were encountered which resulted, for the first time, in a workable, predictable science of the mind and life. New words had to be developed to explain these new phenomena and prevent confusion between Dianetics and older, unworkable schools of the mind. It is a small price to pay to have to learn these new words since they open a whole new frontier of self-betterment for mankind. The Editors □

Do not harken[1] too well to he who would tell you this system will not work. He would not feel safe if people around him grew too strong. The wise man tests before he talks. The critic but follows the fad of a cynical[2] and apathetic age. You have a right to your own opinion. This system works or it doesn't according to your experience. Not all the authorities in Christendom[3] can alter natural law.

---

1. harken: 1. to listen; give heed or attend to what is said.
2. cynical: 1. believing that people are motivated in all their actions only by selfishness; denying the sincerity of people's motives and actions, or the value of living.
3. Christendom: all Christians, Christian countries.

Preface

Get ready.

All by yourself, you're about to do more to help your well-being than you ever thought possible. And all it takes is this book and a half an hour or so a day.

In 1950, author L. Ron Hubbard published *Dianetics: The Modern Science of Mental Health*. Readers—discovering the power of Dianetics to improve themselves—have made the book one of the top best sellers of all time—over 5 million copies sold.

Today, as in 1950, Dianetics spiritual healing technology is a grass-roots phenomenon.

Now, in *Self Analysis*, you can experience the first benefits of Dianetics yourself, in your own home, without a lot of training and without taking up the time of another person.

Just read the opening chapters about you and life (and why the two of you sometimes don't get along). Then start using the lists. They generally ask you to recall—and reenjoy—pleasant moments you've had in the past. What could be more fun? But don't be fooled. Under that apparent simplicity is dynamite—a system that works so well it's been used successfully by millions of people.

You'll probably start feeling the difference in yourself almost as soon as you start doing the processes. So you can actually measure how much of a difference, there are tests on page 55 that let you chart the change in yourself.

Self Analysis—it's quite a book. And it'll help you to prove that you're quite a person!

The Editors

Introduction

*S*_{*elf Analysis* cannot revive the dead.}

Self Analysis will not empty insane asylums or stop war. These are the tasks of the Dianetic auditor[1] and the Group Dianetic Technician.

But *Self Analysis* will conduct you on the most interesting adventure in your life. The adventure of *you*.

How efficient are you? What are your potentials? How much can you improve? Well, basically your intentions toward yourself and your fellow man are *good*. Basically, if sometimes clouded[2] over with the not-so-pale[3] cast[4] of bad experience, your potentialities are a great deal better than anyone ever permitted you to believe.

Take your memory, a small part of your total assets. Is it perfect? Can you, at will, recall everything you have ever learned or heard, every phone number, every name? If you can't you can see that there is room for improvement. Now somebody, with a half-glance at the title page of this book, will try to assume that *Self Analysis* simply improves memory. That is like saying that all a train can do is meet schedules. It does much more. But memory is a starter. If your memory were as accurate as an IBM card[5] index[6] system and

---

1. auditor: the individual who administers Dianetic procedures. To audit means "to listen" and also "to compute."
2. cloud: 11. to overshadow; obscure; darken.
3. pale: 3. not bright or brilliant; dim.
4. cast: 54. a slight tinge of some color; hue; shade.
5. IBM card: a type of paper card that may have information recorded on it by means of punched holes, and which may be read by a computer.
6. index: 2. an ordered list of references to the contents of a larger body of data, such as a file or record, together with the keys or reference notations for identifying, locating, searching or retrieving the contents.

even faster, you would be more efficient and more comfortable and it would certainly save writing those notes you have to make. Yes, you probably couldn't have *too* good a memory on things you've studied and things you need.

But there are a lot of things as important as memory. There's your reaction time. Most people react too slowly in emergencies. Let's say it takes you half a second to pull your hand off a hot stove. That's many times too long a period to have your hand on that stove.

4

Or let's say you require a third of a second to see the car ahead stop and to start to put on your own brakes. That's too long. A lot of accidents happen because of slow reaction time.

In the case of an athlete, reaction time is a direct index[7] as to how capable he may be in a sport. So it assists one in many ways to be able to react quickly.

Self Analysis speeds up reaction time. Here's a trick. Take a dollar bill, unfolded. Have somebody hold it vertically above your hand. Open your thumb and index finger just below the lower edge of the bill. Now let your friend let go. You try to close thumb and index finger on the bill. Did you miss it, snapping after it had gone all the way through? That's very slow reaction. Did you catch it by its upper edge when it was almost gone? That's much too slow. Did you catch it on Washington's face? That's fair. Or did you catch it on the lower edge, even before it really got started? That's the way it should be. Less accidents, greater general alertness. Well, barring actual physical damage to hand or arm, *Self Analysis* will speed that up for you.

Do you have trouble going to sleep or getting up? Do you feel a little tired a lot of the time? Well, that can be remedied.

As for what they call psychosomatic illnesses[8]—sinusitis,[9] allergies, some heart trouble, "bizarre" aches and pains, poor eyesight,

---

7.   index: 4. an indication or sign of something.

8.   psychosomatic illnesses: illnesses which have a mental origin but which are nevertheless organic.

9.   sinusitis: inflammation of a sinus or the sinuses (3b. one of the hollow cavities in the skull connecting with the nasal cavities).

arthritis,[10] etc., etc., etc., down through seventy percent of man's ills, *Self Analysis* should be able to help markedly.

Then there's the matter of how young or old you may look. *Self Analysis* can make quite a change there.

And there's the matter of plain ordinary ability to be happy in life and enjoy things. And there *Self Analysis* shines brightly for it can raise your tone[11] fast enough, usually, so that even you will agree things can be good.

5

As my boyhood hero, Charles Russell,[12] the painter, once described a certain potion,[13] "It'd make a jack rabbit spit in a wolf's eye." Now maybe *Self Analysis* doesn't always have this effect, but it happens regularly enough to be usual. Certain it is that the user often goes through such a period, much to the alarm of his friends. *Self Analysis* does have an effect as in the song:

> I can lick that guy, I can kiss that girl,
> I can ride that bronc and make him whirl. . . .

The moral and caution is "Don't pick too big a wolf." At least not until you've been using this for a while and kind of get things in proportion again.

In short this is an adventure. How good can you get?

A lot depends on how good you are potentially—but you can be assured that that's a lot better than you ever supposed. And it's a cinch it's better than your friends would ever tell you.

Please don't be discouraged if you find yourself pretty low on the self-evaluation chart later on. All is not lost. The processing[14] section can boost you up at a good rate if you keep at it.

---

10. arthritis: a condition causing inflammation, pain and stiffness in the joints.
11. tone: survival potential.
12. Russell, Charles M.: 1864–1926. Artist, writer and cowboy famous for his paintings and stories of cowboy life.
13. potion: a liquid for drinking as a medicine or drug, etc.
14. processing: the principle of making an individual look at his own existence, and improve his ability to confront what he is and where he is.

And don't be surprised if you suddenly begin to feel uncomfortable while you're working on the processing section. You can expect that to happen every now and then. Just keep going. If it gets too bad, simply turn to the last section (page 215) and answer those questions a few times and you should start feeling better very soon.

All I'm trying to tell you is this—adventures are dull if a little excitement doesn't crop up. And you can expect excitement—too much in some places.

6

You are going to know a lot about you when you finally finish.

All this is on your own responsibility. Anything as powerful as these processes can occasionally flare.[15] If you are fairly stable mentally there is no real danger. But I will not mislead you. A man could go mad simply reading this book. If you see somebody who isn't quite as stable as he thinks he is working with *Self Analysis,* coax it away from him. If he can barely stand mental chicken broth, he has no right to be dining on raw meat. Send him to see a Dianetic auditor. And even if he does throw a wheel,[16] a Dianetic auditor can straighten him out. Just send for an auditor.

Don't, then, disabuse[17] yourself of the fact that *Self Analysis* can send the unstable spinning.[18]

We're dealing here with the root stuff of why men go mad. If it isn't explained in the text, it will be found in a standard work on Dianetics. Even so, it is doubtful if *Self Analysis* could create as much madness in a year as an income tax blank from our thorough if somewhat knuckle-headed government.

Now to particulars. You'll find the tests on page 55. You can take the first one. It will give you a figure which will place you on the chart. Don't blame me if it's a low score. Blame your parents or the truant officer.[19]

---

15.   flare: 2a. to cause to flare (*n.* 3. a sudden outburst [as of sound, excitement, or anger]: a flare of temper).
16.   throw a wheel: go into a spin or state of mental confusion.
17.   disabuse: to disillusion (to set free from pleasant but mistaken beliefs), to free from a false idea.
18.   spin: 3. a state of mental confusion.
19.   truant officer: an officer of a public school who investigates absences of pupils.

Next, it would probably interest you to read the text. It will give you a different viewpoint on things, possibly. It is regretted if it is too simple for the savant[20] or too complex or something. It's simply an effort to write in American a few concepts about the mind based on a lot of technical material in Dianetics but made more palatable.[21] You'll do better on the processing if you read the text.

The processing section has a large number of parts. You can simply work straight through or work over each one again, and again, until you feel you've sufficiently explored that part of your life. In any case you will go through every section many times.

7

To help you there is a two-sided disc in the front of the book. The directions are on it.

Thus you are prepared to go exploring into your own life. That's an interesting adventure for anyone. I've done what I could to make it easier. Don't be too harsh on me, however, if you get grounded up some long lost river and eaten by cannibals or engrams.[22] The last section will help get you out. What's left of you, anyway.

Don't get fainthearted and slack off, though, when you find the going rough. It's easy to quit. And then you'd never know just what you really are, basically.

Going to take the whole trip? You're a brave person. I compliment you.

May you never be the same again—

---

20.   savant: a man of profound or extensive learning.
21.   palatable: 2. pleasing or acceptable to the mind or feelings.
22.   engram: a mental image picture which is a recording of a time of physical pain and unconsciousness. It must by definition have impact or injury as part of its content.

8

CHAPTER ONE

On Getting to Know Ourselves

$\mathbf{A}$re you a friend of yours?

9

Probably the most neglected friend you have is you. And yet every man, before he can be a true friend to the world, must first become a friend to himself.

In this society, where aberration[1] flourishes in the crowded cities and marts[2] of business, few are the men who have not been subjected, on every hand, to a campaign to convince them that they are much less than they think they are.

You would fight anyone who said of your friends what is implied about you. It is time you fought for the best friend you will ever have—yourself.

The first move in striking up this friendship is to make an acquaintance[3] with what you are and what you might become. "Know thyself!" said the ancient Greek. Until recently it was not possible to make a very wide acquaintance. Little was known about human behavior as a science. But atomic physics,[4] in revealing new knowledge to man, has also revealed the general characteristics of the energy of life and by that a great deal can be known which was not before suspected. You do not need to know atomic physics to know yourself, but you need to know something of the apparent goal of life[5] in general and your own goals in particular.

In a later chapter there are some questions you can answer which will give you a better insight into your capabilities as they are

---

1. aberration: a departure from rational thought or behavior.
2. mart: 1. a market or trading center.
3. acquaintance: 3. personal knowledge.
4. atomic physics: nuclear physics: the branch of physics that deals with the behavior, structure, and component parts of atomic nuclei (plural of nucleus, 5. the positively charged mass within an atom, composed of neutrons and protons, and possessing most of the mass but occupying only a small fraction of the volume of the atom).
5. goal of life: the goal of life can be considered to be infinite survival. Man, as a life form, can be demonstrated to obey in all his actions and purposes the one command: **"Survive!"**

and what they can become—and do not be deceived, for they can become a great deal more than you ever before suspected.

Just now let's talk about the general goal of all life. Knowing that, we can know something about the basic laws which motivate your own urges and behavior.

All problems are basically simple—once you know the fundamental answer. And this is no exception in life. For thousands of years men strove to discover the underlying drives of existence.[6] And in an enlightened age, when exploration of the universes had already yielded enough secrets to give us A-bombs, it became possible to explore for and find the fundamental law of life. What would you do if you had this fundamental law? How easily then would you understand all the puzzles, riddles and complexities of personality and behavior. You could understand conjurers[7] and bank presidents, colonels and coolies,[8] kings, cats and coal heavers.[9] And more important, you could easily predict what they would do in any given circumstance and you would know what to expect from anyone without any guesswork—indeed with a security diabolical[10] in its accuracy.

"In the beginning was the Word," but what was the word? What fundamental principle did it outline? What understanding would one have if he knew it?

An ancient Persian[11] king once made a great effort to know this word. He tried to discover it by having his sages[12] boil down all the knowledge of the world.

At his orders, every book written which could be obtained was collected together in an enormous library. Books were brought to that ancient city by the caravan load. And the wise men of the time worked for years condensing every piece of knowledge which was known into a single volume.

But the king wanted a better statement of the fundamental word. And he made his sages reduce that volume to a single page.

10

---

6.   existence: an existing state or fact of being; life; living; continuance of being and occurrence; specific manifestation.
7.   conjurer: 2. a magician; sorcerer.
8.   coolie: an unskilled native laborer in the Far East.
9.   coal heaver: a man employed in loading or unloading coal from ships.
10. diabolical: 2. fiendishly clever or cunning or annoying.
11. Persian: of Persia (the ancient and now the alternative name of Iran) or its people or language.
12. sage: a profoundly wise man.

And he made them reduce it again to a sentence. And then, after many more years of study, his philosophers finally obtained that single word, the formula which would solve all riddles.

And the city died in war and the word was lost.

But what was it? Certainly its value, since it would make an understanding of man possible, exceeded the riches of Persia. Two thousand years later, out of the studies of atomic and molecular phenomena, we can again postulate[13] what that word was. And use it. Use it to know ourselves. And to predict the actions of other men.

□   11

---

13.   postulate: to assume (a thing) to be true, especially as a basis for reasoning.

12

CHAPTER TWO

On the Laws of Survival and Abundance

The dynamic[1] principle of existence is: **Survival!**

13

At first glance that may seem too basic. It may seem too simple. But when we examine this word, we find some things about it which make it possible for us to do tricks with it. And to know things which were never known before.

Knowledge could be represented by a pyramid. At the top we would have a simple fact but a fact so widely embracing the universe that many facts could be known from it. From this point we could conceive descending down into greater and greater numbers of facts, represented by the broadening of the pyramid.

At any point we examine this pyramid we would find that as one descended he would find facts of wider and less related meanings. As one went up he would find greater and greater simplicities. Science is the process of starting low on the pyramid, much like the Persian king, and rising up in an effort to discover more basic facts which explain later facts. Philosophy could be said to be the operation of taking very basic facts and then leading them into explanations of greater and greater numbers of facts.

At the point of our pyramid, we have **Survival!**

It is as though, at some remarkably distant time, the Supreme Being gave forth a command to all life: "Survive!" It was not said how to survive nor yet how long. All that was said was "Survive!" The reverse of survive is "succumb."[2] And that is the penalty for not engaging in survival activities.

---

1.   dynamic: 1. relating to energy or physical force in motion.
2.   succumb: the point marked by what one might call the death of the consciousness of the individual.

But what of such things as morals,[3] ideals, love? Don't these things go above "mere survival"? Unfortunately or fortunately, they do not.

When one thinks of survival, one is apt to make the error of thinking in terms of "barest necessity." That is not survival. For it has no margin[4] for loss.

The engineer when he constructs a bridge uses something called a "factor of safety." If a bridge is to hold ten tons, he builds it to hold fifty tons. He makes that bridge five times as strong. Then he has a margin for deterioration of materials, overloading, sudden and unforeseen stress of elements, and any accident which may occur.

In life, the only real guarantee of survival is *abundance*. A farmer who calculates to need twelve bushels[5] of grain for his food for a year and plants twelve bushels has cut back his chances of survival very markedly. The fact is, he will not survive, unless some neighbor has been more prudent.[6] For the grasshoppers will take part of the wheat. And the drought will take some. And the hail will take some. And the tax gatherer will take some. And what will he do for seed wheat if he intends to use all he plants for food?

No, the farmer who knows he has to eat twelve bushels of wheat in the coming year had better plant a hundred. Then the grasshoppers and internal revenue people can chew away as they will. The farmer will still be able to harvest enough for his own food—except of course in a socialism[7] where nobody survives, at least for very long!

An individual survives or succumbs in ratio to his ability to acquire and hold the wherewithal[8] of survival. The security[9] of a good job, for instance, means some guarantee of survival—other threats to existence not becoming too overpowering. The man who makes twenty thousand a year can afford better clothing against the weather, a sounder and better home, medical care for himself and his family, good transportation and, what is important, the respect of his fellows. All these things are survival.

---

3.   morals: 11. principles or habits with respect to right or wrong conduct.
4.   margin: 3. an amount over and above the essential minimum.
5.   bushel: a measure for grain and fruit (32 quarts).
6.   prudent: showing carefulness and foresight, avoiding rashness.
7.   socialism: an ideology which calls for state or government ownership and control of all the means of production and distribution. There is no private enterprise.
8.   wherewithal: the things (especially money) needed for a purpose.
9.   security: 1. the state of being or feeling secure; freedom from fear, anxiety, danger, doubt, etc.; state or sense of safety or certainty.

Of course the man who makes twenty thousand a year can have such a worrisome job, can excite so much envy from his fellows and can be so harassed that he loses something of his survival potential. But even a subversive[10] will change his political coat if you offer him twenty thousand a year.

Take the man who makes ten dollars a week. He wears clothes which protect him very poorly. Thus he can easily become ill. He lives in a place which but ill defends him from the weather. He is haggard[11] with concern. For his level of survival is so low that he has no margin, no abundance. He cannot bank anything against the day he becomes ill. And he cannot pay a doctor. And he can take no vacations. Even in a collective state[12] his lot would be such, his regimentation[13] so thorough that he could do little to protect his own survival.

Youth has a survival abundance over old age. For youth still has endurance. And the dreams of youth—good survival stuff, dreams—are not yet broken by failures. Youth has, in addition, a long expectancy, and that is important, for survival includes length of time to live.

As for ideals, as for honesty, as for one's love of one's fellow man, one cannot find good survival for one or for many where these things are absent. The criminal does not survive well. The average criminal spends the majority of his adult years caged like some wild beast and guarded from escape by the guns of good marksmen. A man who is known to be honest is awarded survival—good jobs, good friends. And the man who has his ideals, no matter how thoroughly the minions[14] of the devil may wheedle[15] him to desert them, survives well only so long as he is true to those ideals. Have you ever heard about a doctor who, for the sake of gain, begins to secretly attend[16] criminals or peddle dope? That doctor does not survive long after his ideals are laid aside.

In short, the most esoteric[17] concepts fall within this understanding of survival. One survives so long as he is true to

15

---

10. subversive: tending or seeking to subvert (1. to overthrow or destroy something established), overthrow, or destroy an established government, institution, belief, etc.—*n.* person regarded as subversive.
11. haggard: looking exhausted and ugly from prolonged worry or illness or lack of sleep.
12. collective (state): 5. organized according to the principles of collectivism (the political principle of centralized social and economic control, especially of all means of production).
13. regiment: 4. to organize in a rigid system under strict discipline and control.
14. minion: 2. a subordinate official, deputy or the like.
15. wheedle: 1. to influence or persuade (a person) by flattery, soothing words, coaxing, etc.
16. attend: 3. to take care of or wait upon; minister to.
17. esoteric: 1b. beyond the understanding or knowledge of most people.

himself, his family, his friends, the laws of the universe. When he fails in any respect, his survival is cut down.

The end of survival, however, is no sharp thing. Survival is not a matter of being alive this moment and dead the next. Survival is actually a graduated scale. □

CHAPTER THREE

On the Death
of Consciousness

Where does one cease to survive and begin to succumb? 17
The point of demarcation[1] is not death as we know it. It is marked
by what one might call the death of the consciousness[2] of the individual.

Man's greatest weapon is his reason.[3] Lacking the teeth,
the armor-plate hide, the claws of so many other life forms, man has
relied upon his ability to reason in order to further himself in his
survival.

The selection of the ability to think as a chief weapon is a
fortunate one. It has awarded man with the kingdom of Earth.
Reason is an excellent weapon. The animal with his teeth, with his
armor-plated hide, with his long claws, is fixed with weapons he
cannot alter. He cannot adjust to a changing environment. And it is
terribly important, to survive, to change when the environment
changes. Every extinct species became extinct because it could not
change to control a new environment. Reason remedies this failure to
a marked extent. For man can invent new tools and new weapons
and a whole new environment. Reason permits him to change to fit
new situations. Reason keeps him in control of new environments.

Any animal that simply adjusts itself to match its environment is doomed. Environments change rapidly. Animals which
control and change the environment have the best chance of survival.

The only way you can organize a collective state is to
convince men that they must adjust and adapt themselves, like
animals, to a constant environment. The people must be deprived of
the right to control, as individuals, their environment. Then they can

---

1.   demarcation: 3. a separation or distinction.
2.   consciousness: awareness of now.
3.   reason: 3. the ability to think, form judgments, draw conclusions, etc.

be regimented and herded into groups. They become owned, not owners. Reason and the right to reason must be taken from them, for the very center of reason is the right to make up one's own mind about one's environment.

The elements fight man and man fights man. The primary target of the enemies of man or a man is his right and ability to reason. The crude and blundering[4] forces of the elements, storms, cold and night bear down against, challenge and then mayhap[5] crush the reason as well as the body.

18   But just as unconsciousness[6] always precedes death, even by instants, so does the death of reason precede the death of the organism. And this action may happen in a long span of time, even half a lifetime, even more.

Have you watched the high alertness of a young man breasting[7] the forces which oppose life? And watched another in old age? You will find that what has suffered has been the ability to reason. He has gained hard-won experience[8] and on this experience he seeks, from middle age on, to travel. It is a truism that youth thinks fast on little experience. And that age thinks slowly on much. The reason of youth is very far from always right, for youth is attempting to reason without adequate data.

Suppose we had a man who had retained all his ability to reason and yet had a great deal of experience. Suppose our graybeards[9] could think with all the enthusiasm and vitality[10] of youth and yet had all their experience as well. Age says to youth, "You have no experience." Youth says to age, "You have no vision,[11] you will not accept or even examine new ideas!" Obviously an ideal arrangement would be for one to have the experience of age and the vitality and vision of youth.

You may have said to yourself, "With all my experience now, what wouldn't I give for some of the enthusiasm I had once." Or perhaps you have excused it all by saying you have "lost your

---

4.   blunder: 2. to move or act blindly, stupidly or without direction or steady guidance.
5.   mayhap: perhaps; maybe.
6.   unconsciousness: a condition wherein the organism is discoordinated only in its analytical process and motor control direction.
7.   breast: 2. to face or meet firmly; move forward against.
8.   experience: 1. actual observation of facts or events, activity or practice in doing something.
9.   graybeard: an old man.
10.   vitality: 4. mental or physical vigor; energy.
11.   vision: 3. imaginative insight into a subject or problem, etc., foresight and wisdom in planning.

illusions."[12] But you aren't sure that they were illusions. Are brightness in life, quick enthusiasm, a desire and will to live, a belief in destiny, are these things illusions? Or are they symptoms[13] of the very stuff of which vital life is made? And isn't their decline a symptom of death?

Knowledge[14] does not destroy a will to live. Pain and loss of self-determinism[15] destroy that will. Life can be painful. The gaining of experience is often painful. The retaining of that experience is essential. But isn't it still experience if it doesn't yet have the pain?

19

Suppose you could wipe out of your life all the pain, physical and otherwise, which you have accumulated. Would it be so terrible to have to part with a broken heart or a psychosomatic illness, with fears and anxieties and dreads?

Suppose a man had a chance again, with all he knows, to look life and the universe in the eye again and say it could be whipped. Do you recall a day, when you were younger, and you woke to find bright dew sparkling on the grass, the leaves, to find the golden sun bright upon a happy world? Do you recall how beautiful and fine it once was? The first sweet kiss? The warmth of true friendship? The intimacy[16] of a moonlight ride? What made it become otherwise than a brilliant world?

The consciousness of the world around one is not an absolute thing. One can be more conscious of color and brightness and joy at one time of life more than another. One can more easily feel the brilliant reality of things in youth than he can in age. And isn't this something like a decline of consciousness, of awareness?[17]

What is it that makes one less aware of the brilliance of the world around him? Has the world changed? No, for each new generation sees the glamour and the glory, the vitality of life—the same life that age may see as dull at best. The individual changes. And what makes him change? Is it a decay of his glands[18] and

---

12.   illusion: any idea, space, energy, object or time concept which one creates himself.
13.   symptom: any circumstance, event, or condition that accompanies something and indicates its existence or occurrence; sign; indication.
14.   knowledge: by knowledge we mean assured belief, that which is known information, instruction; enlightenment, learning; practical skill. By knowledge we mean data, factors and whatever can be thought about or perceived.
15.   self-determinism: means the ability to direct himself.
16.   intimacy: 2. a close, familiar, and usually affectionate or loving, personal relationship.
17.   awareness: the ability to perceive the existence of.
18.   gland: an organ that secretes substances that are to be used by the body or expelled from it.

sinews?[19] Hardly, for all the work that has been done on glands and sinews—the structure of the body—has restored little if any of the brilliance of living.

Ah, youth, sighs the adult, if I but had your zest[20] again! What reduced that zest?

As one's consciousness of the brilliance of life declines, so has declined his own consciousness. Awareness decreases exactly as consciousness decreases. The ability to perceive the world around one and the ability to draw accurate conclusions about it are, to all intents, the same thing.

Glasses are a symptom of the decline of consciousness. One needs his sight bolstered to make the world look brighter. The loss of the ability to move swiftly, as one ran when he was a child, is a decline of consciousness and ability.

Complete unconsciousness is death. Half unconsciousness is half death. A quarter unconsciousness is a quarter of death. And as one accumulates the pain attendant[21] upon life and fails to accumulate the pleasures, one gradually loses his race with the gentleman with the scythe.[22] And there ensues, at last, the physical incapacity for seeing, thinking and being, known as death.

How does one accumulate this pain? And if he got rid of it would full consciousness and a full bright concept[23] of life return? And is there a way to get rid of it?   □

---

19.   sinews: 1. tough fibrous tissue uniting muscle to bone.
20.   zest: 2. stimulating or exciting quality; flavor.
21.   attendant: 3. accompanying as a circumstance or result.
22.   gentleman with the scythe: grim reaper: death, especially when personified as a man or skeleton with a scythe.
23.   concept: that which is retained after something has been perceived.

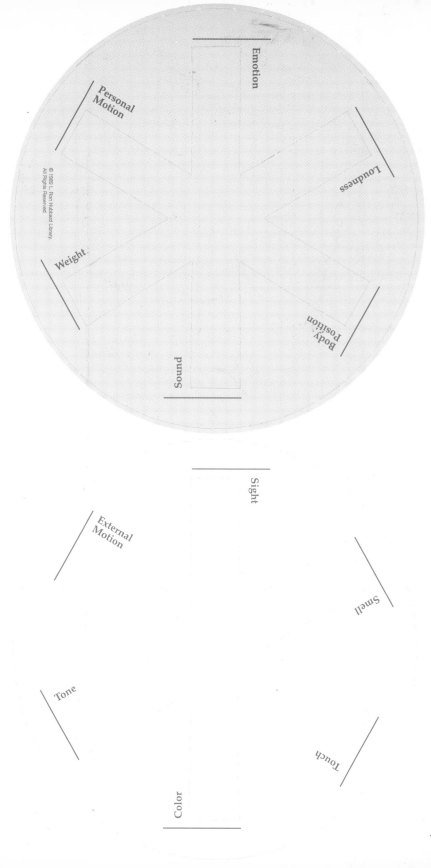

Emotion

Personal
Motion

Loudness

© 1989 L. Ron Hubbard Library.
All Rights Reserved.

Weight

Body
Position

Sound

Sight

External
Motion

Smell

Tone

Touch

Color

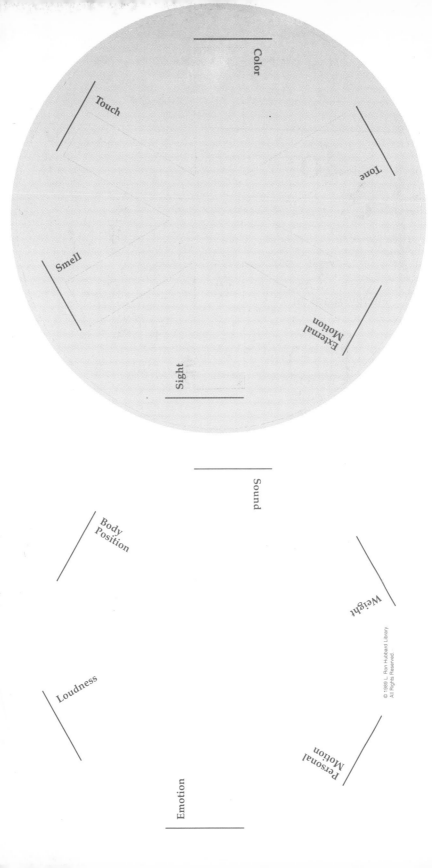

Color

Touch

Tone

Smell

External
Motion

Sight

Sound

Body
Position

Weight

Loudness

Personal
Motion

Emotion

CHAPTER FOUR

On Our Efforts for Immortality

The physical universe[1] consists of four elements—matter, energy, space and time.

According to nuclear physics, matter is composed of energy such as electrons[2] and protons.[3] And the energy and the matter exist in space and time. All this is actually very simple. And even then we need not go very far into it to understand that the universe in which we live is composed of simple things arranged and rearranged to make many forms and manifestations.[4]

The concrete sidewalk, the air, ice cream sodas, paychecks, cats, kings and coal heavers are basically composed of matter, energy, space and time. And where they are alive they contain another ingredient—life.

Life is an energy of a very special kind, obeying certain laws different from what we normally consider energy such as electricity. But life is an energy and it has some peculiar properties.

Life is able to collect and organize matter and energy in space and time and animate[5] it. Life takes some matter and energy and makes an organism such as a monocell,[6] a tree, a polar bear or a man. Then this organism, still animated by the energy called life, further acts upon matter and energy in space and time and further organizes and animates matter and energy into new objects and shapes.

---

1. physical universe: the universe of matter, energy, space and time. It would be the universe of the planets, their rocks, rivers and oceans, the universe of stars and galaxies, the universe of burning suns and time.
2. electron: a particle of matter with a negative electric charge.
3. proton: a particle of matter with a positive electric charge.
4. manifestation: 2. the state of being manifested (readily perceived by the eye or the understanding; evident; obvious; apparent; plain).
5. animate: 1. to give life to; make alive.
6. monocell: an organism composed of a single cell.

Life could be said to be engaged upon a conquest of the physical universe. The primary urge of life has been said to be survival. In order to accomplish survival, life has to continue and win in its conquest of the physical universe.

When life or a life form ceases to continue that conquest, it ceases to survive and succumbs.

Here we have a gigantic action. The energy of life versus[7] matter, energy, space and time.

22   Life versus the physical universe.

Here is an enormous struggle. The chaotic, disorganized physical universe, capable only of force, resisting the conquest of life, organizing and persistent, capable of reason.

Life learns the laws of the physical universe matter, energy, space and time and then turns those laws against the physical universe to further its conquest.

Man has spent much time learning what he could of the physical universe as in the sciences of physics[8] and chemistry[9] but, more important even, of the daily battle of life against the universe. Do not think that a monocell does not manifest a knowledge of life's working rules, for it does. What cunning[10] it takes to organize some chemicals and sunlight into a living unit! The biologist[11] stands in awe of the expertness of management of the smallest living cells. He gazes at these intricate and careful entities, these microscopic units of life forms, and even he cannot believe that it is all an accident.

There is life, then, a vital energy, not quite like physical universe energy. And then there are life forms. The life form or the organism, such as a living human body, consists of life *plus* physical universe matter, energy, space and time. A *dead* body consists of physical universe matter, energy, space and time *minus* life energy. Life has been there, has organized and has then withdrawn from the organism, an operation we know as the cycle of conception, birth, growth, decay and death.

---

7.   versus: 1. in contest against.

8.   physics: 1. the scientific study of the properties and interactions of matter and energy.

9.   chemistry: 1. the scientific study of substances and their elements and of how they react when combined or in contact with one another.

10.   cunning: 3. made or done with skill or ingenuity.

11.   biologist: an expert in biology (the scientific study of life and structure of living things).

Although there are answers as to where life goes when it withdraws and what it then does, we need not examine that now. The important thing to a living organism is the fact that it is seeking to survive, in obedience to the whole effort of all life, and that in order to do so it must succeed in its conquest of the physical universe.

Stated simply, life must first accumulate enough matter and energy to make up an organism—such as the human body—and must then ally[12] the organism with friendly and cooperative organisms—such as other people—and must continue to procure additional matter and energy for food, clothing and shelter in order to support itself. Additionally, in order to survive, it must do two specific things which, beyond the necessity of allies, food, clothing and shelter, are basically important.

Life must procure pleasure.[13]

Life must avoid pain.

Life has an active thrust away from pain, which is non-survival, destructive and which is death itself. Pain is a warning of nonsurvival or potential death.

Life has an active thrust toward pleasure. Pleasure can be defined as the action toward obtaining or the procurement of survival. The ultimate pleasure is an infinity of survival or immortality, a goal unobtainable for the physical organism itself (but not its life), but toward which the organism strives.

Happiness then could be defined as the overcoming of obstacles toward a desirable goal. Any desirable goal, if closely inspected, will be found to be a survival goal.

Too much pain obstructs the organism toward survival.

Too many obstructions between the organism and survival mean nonsurvival.

Thus one finds the mind[14] engaged in computing or imagining ways and means to avoid pain and reach pleasure and putting the solutions into action. And this is all that the mind does: it

23

12.   ally: 2. to associate or connect by some mutual relationship.
13.   pleasure: the Dianetic definition of pleasure is that the organism tending toward survival obtains pleasure by survival actions and the seeking of survival goals.
14.   mind: is the command post of operation and is constructed to resolve problems and pose problems related to survival and only to survival.

perceives, poses[15] and resolves problems[16] relating to the survival of the organism, the future generations, the group, life and the physical universe and puts the solutions into action. If it solves the majority of the problems presented, the organism thus achieves a high level of survival. If the organism's mind fails to resolve a majority of problems, then the organism fails.

The mind, then, has a definite relationship to survival. And one means here the whole mind, not just the brain. The brain is a structure. The mind can be considered to be the whole being, mortal and immortal, the definite personality of the organism and all its attributes.

Hence, if one's mind is working well, if it is resolving the problems it should resolve and if it is putting those solutions into proper action, the survival of the organism is well assured. If the mind is not working well, the survival of the organism is thrown into question and doubt.

One's mind, then, must be in excellent condition if he is to best guarantee the survival of himself, his family, future generations, his group and life.

The mind seeks to guarantee and direct survival actions. It seeks survival not only for the organism (self) but seeks it for the family, children, future generations and all life. Thus it can be selectively blunted.[17]

A mind can be blunted concerning the survival of self and yet be alive to the survival of future generations. It can be blunted concerning groups and yet be very alive to its responsibility for the organism (self). In order to function well, the mind must not be blunted in any direction.

To function well the mind must conceive itself able to handle the physical universe of matter, energy, space and time within the necessities of the organism, the family, future generations and groups as well as life.

The mind must be able to avoid pain for and discover pleasure for the self, future generations, the family and the group as well as life itself.

24

---

15.   pose: 1. to examine by questioning, question, interrogate.
16.   problem: the definition of a problem is intention versus intention or two or more opposing or conflicting views on the same subject.
17.   blunt: 3. to make less effective.

As the mind fails to avoid pain and discover pleasure, so fails the organism, the family, future generations, the group and life.

The failure of one organism in a group to properly resolve survival problems is a failure, in part, for the whole group. Hence, "Do not send to find for whom the bell tolls;[18] it tolls for thee!"

Life is an interdependent,[19] cooperative effort. Each and every living organism has a·part to play in the survival of other organisms.

When it comes to a thinking mind such as man's, the organism must be able to act independently for its own survival and the survival of others. In order to accomplish these survivals, however, a mind has to be able to realize solutions which are optimum not only for self but for all other things concerned in its survival.

25

Thus the mind of one organism must reach agreements with the minds of other organisms in order that all may survive to the highest possible level.

When a mind becomes dulled and blunted, it begins to compute its solutions poorly. It begins to get confused about its goals. It is not sure what it really means to do. And it will involve and inhibit the survival of other organisms. It may begin, for instance, to compute that it must survive as self and that only self is important and so neglect the survival of others. This is nonsurvival activity. It is highly aberrated.

A mind which begins to "survive" only for self and begins to diminish and control with force other organisms around is already better than halfway toward its own death. It is a mind which is less than half alive. It has less than half its actual potential. Its perception of the physical universe is poor. It does not realize that it is dependent for survival upon cooperation with others. It has lost its survival mission. This mind is already outward bound toward death, has passed its peak and will actually take personal actions which lead to its own death.

18.   toll: 2a. to ring (a church bell, etc.) slowly with regularly repeated strokes, especially for announcing a death.
19.   interdependent: dependent on each other.

Life, the large overall life, has a use for organism death. When an organism can no longer continue well, the plan of life is to kill it and invest anew in a new organism.

Death is life's operation of disposing of an outmoded[20] and unwanted organism so that new organisms can be born and can flourish.

Life itself does not die. Only the physical organism dies. Not even a personality,[21] apparently, dies. Death then, in truth, is a limited concept of the death of the physical part of the organism. Life and the personality, apparently, go on. The physical part of the organism ceases to function. And that is death.

When an organism reaches a point where it is only half conscious, where it is only perceiving half as well as it should, where it is functioning only half as well as it should, death begins. The organism, thereafter, will take actions to hasten death. It does this "unconsciously." But, in its aberrated state, such a mind will also bring death to other organisms. Thus a half conscious organism is a menace to others.

Here is the accident prone, the fascist,[22] the person who seeks to dominate, the selfish and self-seeking person. Here is an organism outward bound.

When an organism reaches a point where it is only a third alive, a third conscious, it is perceiving only a third of what it might, life even further hastens the death of this organism and those around it. Here is the suicide, here is the person who is continually ill, who refuses to eat.

Organisms which are outward bound toward death sometimes require years and years to die. For the organism experiences resurgences[23] and still has some small desire to go on living. And other organisms help it to live. It is carried along by the tide of life even though its individual direction is toward death—death for others and death for self and death for the physical universe around it.

---

20.   outmoded: 2. not acceptable by present standards; no longer usable; obsolete.
21.   personality: the individual, the personality, is the awareness of awareness unit, and the awareness of awareness unit is the person.
22.   fascist: 2. a person who believes in or practices fascism (2. a system of government characterized by rigid one-party dictatorship, forcible suppression of opposition, private economic enterprise under centralized governmental control, belligerent nationalism, racism, and militarism, etc.).
23.   resurgent: rising or tending to rise again; reviving.

26

Society, the bulk of which is bent upon survival, fails or refuses to recognize death or the urge of organisms toward it. Society passes laws against murder and suicide. Society provides hospitals. Society carries such people upon its back. And society will not hear of euthanasia or "mercy killing."

Organisms which have passed the halfway point will take extraordinary measures and means to bring about death for others and for things and for self. Here we have the Hitlers, the criminals, the destructively neurotic.[24]

Give a person who has passed this point a car to drive and the car may become involved in an accident. Give him money and the money will go to purchase nonsurvival things.

27

But we must not emphasize the dramatic and forget the important like the newspapers do. The action and urge toward death becomes noticeable only when it is very dramatic. It is most dangerous however in its undramatic forms.

A person who has passed the halfway point brings death to things and people on a small scale at all times. A house left dirty, appointments not kept, clothing not cared for, vicious gossip, carping[25] criticisms of others "for their own good": these are all enturbulences which bring failure and too many failures bring death.

And it should be not supposed that by halfway point one means halfway through life. It means half conscious, half alive, half or less perceiving and thinking. A child may be suppressed[26] to this level by his parents and school. And indeed children quite ordinarily drop below the halfway point, so defeated do they become in their environment and in their contest with life. Age is no criterion.[27] But physical health is.

The surest manifestation that someone has passed the halfway point is his physical condition. The chronically ill have passed it.

If one is to have a secure society, then, if one is to rid a society of its death factors, one must have some means of either

---

24. neurotic: a person who is mainly harmful to himself by reason of his aberrations, but not to the point of suicide.
25. carp: to keep finding fault, to raise petty objections.
26. suppress: to squash, to sit on, to make smaller, to refuse to let reach, to make uncertain about his reaching, to render or lessen in any way possible by any means possible.
27. criterion: a standard of judgment.

destroying the people who bring death to it, the Hitlers, the insane, the criminals, or he must have some means of salvaging these people and bringing them back into a state of full consciousness.

Full consciousness would mean full recognition of one's responsibilities, his relationship with others, his care of himself and of society.

28

How can such a thing be achieved? If you could achieve it, you could raise a social order to hitherto[28] unattainable heights. You could empty the prisons and insane asylums. You could make a world too sane for war. And people could be made well who have never had the means of it before. And people could be happy who have never truly known what happiness was. You could raise the good will and efficiency of all men and all social orders if you could restore the vitality of these people.

In order to know how it can be restored, one has to know how the consciousness, the vitality, the will to live become reduced.

□

---

28.   hitherto: until this time.

CHAPTER FIVE

On Raising Our Level of Consciousness

An organism is suppressed toward death by accumulated pain.

Pain in one great sweeping shock[1] brings about immediate death.

Pain in small doses over a lifetime gradually suppresses the organism toward death.

What is pain?

Pain is the warning of loss. It is an automatic alarm system built into life organisms which informs the organism that some part of it or all of it is under stress and that the organism had better take action or die.

The signal of pain means that the organism is in the proximity[2] of a destructive force or object. To ignore pain is to die. Pain is the whip which sends the organism away from hot stoves, sub-zero weather; pain is the threat of nonsurvival, the punishment for errors in trying to survive.

And pain is always loss. A burned finger means that the body has lost the cells on the surface of that finger. They are dead. A blow on the head means the death of scalp and other cells in the area. The whole organism is thus warned of the proximity of a death source and so attempts to get away from it.

The loss of a loved one is also a loss of survival. The loss of a possession is also loss of survival potential. One then confuses physical pain and the loss of survival organisms or objects. And so there is such a thing as "mental pain."

---

1. shock: a person can be broken down on the emotional scale so steeply, sharply and suddenly that they can be killed. That's what's known as shock.
2. proximity: 1. nearness.

But life, in its whole contest with the physical universe, has no patience with failure. An organism so foolhardy as to let itself be struck too hard and so depressed into unconsciousness stays in the vicinity of the pain-dealing object. It is considered to be nonsurvival if it fails so markedly to survive.

Unconsciousness experienced as a result of a blow or an illness is a quick picture of what happens over a life span.

Is there any difference except time between these two things?

30

A blow resulting in unconsciousness which results in death.

The accumulated blows over a life span resulting in a gradual lessening of consciousness resulting in eventual death.

One is slower than the other.

One of the basic discoveries of Dianetics was that unconsciousness and all the pain attendant upon it was stored in a part of the mind and that this pain and unconsciousness accumulated until it caused the organism to begin to die.

Another discovery of Dianetics was that this pain could be nullified[3] or erased with a return to full consciousness and a rehabilitation toward survival.

In other words, with Dianetics, it became possible to cancel out the accumulated unconsciousness and pain of the years and restore the health and vitality of an organism.

Accumulated physical pain and loss brings about a reduction of consciousness, a reduction of physical health and a reduction of the will to live to a point where the organism actively, if often slyly, seeks death.

Erase or nullify the physical pain, the losses of a lifetime, and vitality returns.

The vitality of living, of seeking higher levels of survival, is life itself.

---

3.   nullify: 3. to cancel out.

The human body was found to be extremely capable of repairing itself when the stored memories of pain were cancelled. Further it was discovered that so long as the stored pain remained, the doctoring of what are called psychosomatic ills, such as arthritis, rheumatism,[4] dermatitis[5] and thousands of others, could not result in anything permanent. Psychotherapy,[6] not knowing about pain storage and its effects, discovered long ago that one could rid a patient of one illness only to have another pop up—and psychotherapy became a defeatist[7] school because it could do nothing permanent for the aberrated or the ill even when it could do a little something to relieve it. Hence, all efforts to make men vital and well became suspect because the reason they were inefficient and ill had not been discovered and proven.

31

With Dianetics it became possible to eradicate[8] aberration and illness because it became possible to nullify or eradicate the pain from the pain-storage banks of the body without applying further pain as in surgery.

Consciousness then depends upon the absence or the nullification or eradication of memories of physical pain, for unconsciousness is a part of that pain—one of its symptoms.

Arthritis of the knee, for instance, is the accumulation of all knee injuries in the past. The body confuses time and environment with the time and environment where the knee was actually injured and so keeps the pain there. The fluids of the body avoid the pain area. Hence a deposit which is called arthritis. The proof of this is that when the knee injuries of the past are located and discharged,[9] the arthritis ceases, no other injury takes its place and the person is finished with arthritis of the knee. And this happens ten cases out of ten—except in those cases where age and physical deterioration are so well advanced toward death that the point of no-return is passed.

Take a bad heart. The person has pain in his heart. He can take medicine or voodoo[10] or another diet and still have a bad heart. Find and eradicate or nullify an actual physical injury to the heart and the heart ceases to hurt and gets well.

---

4. rheumatism: any of several diseases causing pain in the joints or muscles or fibrous tissue.
5. dermatitis: inflammation of the skin.
6. psychotherapy: treatment of mental disorders by the use of psychological (1. of or affecting the mind or its workings) methods.
7. defeatist: a person who expects to be defeated or accepts defeat too easily.
8. eradicate: 2. to get rid of; wipe out; destroy.
9. discharged: erased.
10. voodoo: a form of religion based on a belief in witchcraft and magical rites, practiced by some people in the West Indies and America.

Nothing is easier to prove than these tenets.[11] A good Dianetic auditor can take a broken-down, sorrow-drenched lady of thirty-eight and knock out her past periods of physical and mental pain and have on his hands somebody who appears to be twenty-five—and a bright, cheerful twenty-five at that.

Sure it's incredible. But so is an A-bomb, a few penny-weights[12] of plutonium[13] which can blow a city off the chart.

Once you know the basic tenets of life and how it acts as an energy, life can be put back into the ill, the devitalized, the would-be suicide.

32

And more important than treating the very ill, mentally or physically, one can interrupt the downward spiral in a man who is still alert and well so that he will not thereafter become so ill. And one can take the so-called "normal" person and send his state of being up to levels of brilliance and success not possible before.

Restore an individual's full consciousness and you restore his full life potential.

And it can now be done.   □

---

11.   tenet: a firm belief or principle or doctrine of a person or group.
12.   pennyweight: a measure of weight equal to 1/20 of an ounce in troy weight (a system of weights used for precious metals and gems, where there are twelve ounces to a normal pound).
13.   plutonium: a radioactive chemical element, used in nuclear weapons and reactors.

CHAPTER SIX

On Raising Our Level of Life and Behavior

$\mathbf{T}$he tone scale, a small edition of which is in this book (page 44), plots the descending spiral of life from full vitality and consciousness through half vitality and half consciousness down to death.

33

By various calculations about the energy of life, by observation and by test, this tone scale is able to give levels of behavior as life declines.

These various levels are common to all men.

When a man is nearly dead, he can be said to be in a chronic[1] *apathy*. And he behaves in a certain way about other things. This is 0.1 on the tone scale chart.

When a man is chronically in *grief* about his losses, he is in grief. And he behaves certain ways about many things. This is 0.5 on the chart.

When a person is not yet so low as grief but realizes losses are impending, or is fixed chronically at this level by past losses, he can be said to be in *fear*. This is around 1.1 on the chart.

An individual who is fighting against threatened losses is in *anger*. And he manifests other aspects of behavior. This is 1.5.

The person who is merely suspicious that loss may take place or who has become fixed at this level is resentful. He can be said to be in *antagonism*. This is 2.0 on the chart.

Above antagonism, the situation of a person is not so good that he is enthusiastic, not so bad that he is resentful. He has lost

---

1.   chronic: 1. affecting a person for a long time.

some goals and cannot immediately locate others. He is said to be in *boredom*, or at 2.5 on the tone scale chart.

At 3.0 on the chart, a person has a *conservative*, cautious aspect toward life but is reaching his goals.

At 4.0 the individual is *enthusiastic*, happy and vital.

Very few people are natural 4.0s. A charitable[2] average is probably around 2.8.

34

You can examine the chart and you will find in the boxes, as you go across it, the various characteristics of people at these levels. Horribly enough these characteristics have been found to be constant. If you have a 3.0 as your rating, then you will carry across the whole chart at 3.0.

You have watched this chart in operation before now. Have you ever seen a child trying to acquire, let us say, a nickel? At first he is happy. He simply wants a nickel. If refused, he then explains why he wants it. If he fails to get it and did not want it badly, he becomes bored and goes away. But if he wants it badly, he will get antagonistic about it. Then he will become angry. Then, that failing, he may lie about why he wants it. That failing he goes into grief. And if he is still refused, he finally sinks into apathy and says he doesn't want it. This is negation.[3]

And you have seen the chart in reverse. A child threatened by danger also dwindles down the scale. At first he does not appreciate[4] that the danger is posed[5] at him and he is quite cheerful. Then the danger, let us say it is a dog, starts to approach him. The child sees the danger but still does not believe it is for him and keeps on with his business. But his playthings "bore" him for the moment. He is a little apprehensive and not sure. Then the dog comes nearer. The child "resents him" or shows some antagonism. The dog comes nearer still. The child becomes angry and makes some effort to injure the dog. The dog comes still nearer and is more threatening. The child becomes afraid. Fear unavailing,[6] the child cries. If the dog still threatens him, the child may go into an apathy and simply wait to be bitten.

---

2.   charitable: 2. kindly or lenient in judging people, acts, etc.
3.   negate: to nullify, to disprove.
4.   appreciate: 3. to understand.
5.   pose: 1. to place in a specific position.
6.   unavailing: achieving nothing, ineffectual.

Objects or animals or people which assist survival, as they become inaccessible to the individual, bring him down the tone scale.

Objects, animals or people which threaten survival, as they approach the individual, bring him down the tone scale.

This scale has a chronic or an acute[7] aspect. A person can be brought down the tone scale, to a low level for ten minutes and then go back up, or he can be brought down it for ten years and not go back up.

A man who has suffered too many losses, too much pain, tends to become fixed at some lower level of the scale and, with only slight fluctuations, stays there. Then his general and common behavior will be at that level of the tone scale.

Just as a 0.5 moment of grief can cause a child to act along the grief band for a short while, so can a 0.5 fixation cause an individual to act 0.5 toward most things in his life.

There is momentary behavior or fixed behavior.

How can one find an individual on this tone scale? How can one find oneself?

If you can locate two or three characteristics along a certain level of this scale, you can look in the number column opposite those characteristics and find the level. It may be 2.5, it may be 1.5. Wherever it is, simply look at *all* the columns opposite the number you found and you will see the remaining characteristics.

The only mistake you can make in evaluating somebody else on this tone scale is to assume that he departs from it somewhere and is higher in one department than he is in another. The characteristic may be masked to which you object—but it is there.

Look at the top of the first column and you get a general picture of the behavior and physiology[8] of the person. Look at the second column for the physical condition. Look at the third column for the most generally expressed emotion[9] of the person. Continue on

35

---

7.   acute: 4. (of disease) brief and severe.
8.   physiology: 2. the organic processes or functions of an organism or any of its parts.
9.   emotion: emotion could be called the energy manifestation of affinity. As used in Dianetics, emotion could be called the index of the state of being. In the English language, "emotional" is often considered synonymous with "irrational." This would seem to assume that if one is emotional one cannot be reasonable. No more unreasonable assumption could possibly be made.

across the various columns. Somewhere you will find data about somebody or yourself of which you can be sure. Then simply examine all the other boxes at the level of the data you were certain about. That band, be it 1.5 or 3.0, will tell you the story of a human being.

Of course, as good news and bad, happy days and sad ones, strike a person, there are momentary raises and lowerings on this tone scale. But there is a chronic level, an average behavior for each individual.

36

As an individual is found lower and lower on this chart, so is his alertness, his consciousness lower and lower.

The individual's chronic mood or attitude toward existence declines in direct ratio to the way he regards the physical universe and organisms about him.

There are many other mechanical aspects of this chart having to do with energy manifestations and observation of behavior but we need not cover them here.

It is not a complete statement to say, merely, that one becomes fixed in his regard for the physical universe and organisms about him, for there are definite ways, beyond consciousness, which permit this to take place. Manifestation, however, is a decline of consciousness with regard to the physical environment of an individual. That decline of consciousness is a partial cause of a gradual sag down this chart, but it is illustrative enough for our purposes in this volume.

At the top of this chart, one is fully conscious of himself, his environment, other people and the universe in general. He accepts his responsibilities in it. He faces the realities of it. He deals with the problems within the limits of his education and experience.

Then something happens—his perception of the material universe is dulled. How does this come about?

The first and foremost way that a decline on the chart is begun is through being caused physical pain by the physical universe. It is one thing to gain experience and quite another to suffer physical pain. For any experience surrounded by actual physical pain is *hidden* by that pain. The organism is supposed to avoid pain to survive. It avoids, as well, memories of pain if it is above 2.0 on the chart. It "relishes" pain memories below 2.0 as these lead to death. As soon as it can begin avoiding pain wholesale,[10] although that pain is recorded, consciousness begins to decrease markedly. The perception of the physical universe begins to decrease and the caliber[11] of one's activities begins to decline.

One could say that there is an interior world and an exterior world. The interior world is the one of yesterday. The data it contains is used to judge the world of the exterior, of today and tomorrow. So long as one has all data available, one can make excellent computations. When the facts he has learned begin to be buried, one's conclusions are apt to become wrong to just that degree.

37

As one's confidence in the physical universe declines, so does one's ability to handle it decline. One's dreams and hopes begin to seem unattainable, one ceases to strive. Actually, however, one's ability seldom diminishes—it only *seems* to diminish.

When the interior world tells of too much physical pain, the organism becomes confused. Like the child who finally says he doesn't want the nickel, the organism says it wants nothing of the physical universe and so perishes—or lives a while in a twilight and then perishes all the same.

The goal is to win. When one has lost too much and too many times, the possibility of winning *seems* too remote to try. And it loses. It becomes so accustomed to loss that it begins to concentrate on loss instead of forward advance. And it does this quite irrationally. Because one has lost two cars does not mean one may lose three, yet he who has lost two will actually be so prepared to lose three that he will actually, if unconsciously, take steps to lose the third. Thus it may be with people, with any object.

As an individual descends the tone scale, he first begins to lose his confidence in trying to reach the further rims of his environment, the further frontiers of his dreams, and becomes "conservative." There is not much wrong with cautiousness, but there is something wrong with chronic conservatism for sometimes it takes a wild charge to win a life.

As physical pain begins to mount up in the recording banks of the mind, the individual further confuses yesterday with today and further withdraws his confidence. He becomes a little frightened and poses as being bored—he says he didn't want to reach

---

10.　wholesale: 2. extensively, sweepingly or indiscriminately.
11.　caliber: 3. ability, importance.

so far anyway. Isn't worth it. He makes fun of the things he really wants, makes fun of the dreams of others and acts, in general, like a reporter from the *New Yorker*.[12] He is afraid to face a hopeful fact, much less a truly desirable object.

With a further increase of pain, he continues on down the scale until he is actually on his way out from life.

38

The fact of the matter is, the older a person gets and the more experiences he has, the better able he should be to handle his environment. If he could stay fully conscious and rational about it, this would be true. But the mechanics of pain storage are such that he actually grows less and less conscious the more pain he has received and so cannot really use his experience at all. If he could gain experience without physical pain, his enthusiasm, his ability and dash would remain very high. But man was a lesser organism, evidently, before he was a man. And a lesser organism can only react, it cannot think. Thinking is something new.

Until Dianetics, this looked like a hopelessly closed cycle. One had enthusiasm but no experience. So with enthusiastic rushes he attacked the environment with all the folly of youth and was ignominiously[13] repelled. He gained pain with each repulsion. He gained experience, but he could not think about the experience without facing the pain so the experience did him no good. When he had enough experience he no longer had the dreams, energy and enthusiasm to carry home his attack upon his environment.

Processing such as the questions in the last section of this book or in Dianetic co-auditing[14] broke the cycle. Youth could attack the environment and experience pain of repulsion. But the physical pain could be knocked out of the mind by Dianetics, leaving the experience standing there, *with* the enthusiasm.

There must be, at this writing, tens of thousands of people who have experienced Dianetics by now. A few, here and there, were unable to achieve full benefit because it formerly required considerable technical knowledge to process somebody. This book and Self Analysis were developed in order that an individual could gain at least the primary benefits of processing without any technical knowledge and without taking up the time of another person.

---

12.   New Yorker: a literary magazine in New York containing book and theater criticism.
13.   ignominious: bringing contempt or disgrace, humiliating.
14.   co-auditing: is an abbreviation for cooperative auditing. It means a team of any two people who are helping each other reach a better life.

Wherever a person may be on the tone scale (unless he is very low and in the insane bracket, for this is also a scale of sanity) he can ascend that scale again by rehabilitating his ability to think about and know his environment. Now that one knows the rules it is rather easily done and one is astonished that it could not be done before.

Have you looked at the chart for yourself? Well, don't go looking for a cliff or an axe if you were below 2.0. Self Analysis can pull you up this chart so that even you will see that you have climbed.

Now, just beyond the chart there are some tests and graphs. You should answer these. They will help you to locate yourself. Then you will know much better why you are or aren't a good friend to yourself. You may find you don't care to have such a friend. Well, if he's that bad off, he really needs your help. So give him a hand. The whole last part of the book is filled with exercises which will make a better friend to have out of yourself if you just apply these exercises a half an hour a day.

I don't know how high you can get yourself up on this chart. You can raise yourself pretty far and Dianetic co-auditing can do the rest if you wish. Or you may get all the way and stabilize there.

Right now if you aren't being a friend of yourself, I'm your friend. I know by experience that you can climb the chart.

Man is basically good. Pain and social aberrations turn him away from high ethics,[15] efficiency and happiness. Get rid of the pain and you'll be at the high level of the chart.

Now turn to the questions which will help you locate yourself. **But don't use this chart as an effort to make somebody knuckle under.[16] Don't tell people where they are on it. It may ruin them. Let them take their own examinations.** □

---

15.   ethics: ethics are the actions an individual takes on himself in order to accomplish optimum survival for himself and others. Ethical conduct includes the adherence to the moral codes of the society in which we live.

16.   knuckle under: 8b. to submit, yield.

40

CHAPTER SEVEN

The Hubbard Chart of Human Evaluation

This chart is a specialized form of the Hubbard Chart of   41
Human Evaluation and Dianetic Processing.

A full description of each column on this chart (except the last six which are only in *Self Analysis*) will be found complete in *Science of Survival*, a book on the prediction of human behavior by L. Ron Hubbard.

The position of an individual on this tone scale varies through the day and throughout the years but is fairly stable for given periods. One's position on the chart will rise on receipt of good news, sink with bad news. This is the usual give and take with life. Everyone however has a *chronic* position on the chart which is unalterable save for processing.

Necessity level (lifting oneself by one's bootstraps as in emergencies) can raise an individual well up this chart for brief periods.

By education, such as that given under pressure, the education itself has a position on the tone scale. A person could be relatively unaberrated actually but, by education, be at a lower position on the chart than he should be. The reverse is also the case. One can be educated, then, into a higher or lower level on the chart than his own aberrations call for.

One's environment greatly influences one's position on the chart. Every environment has its own tone level. A man who is really a 3.0 can begin to act like a 1.1 in a 1.1 environment. However, a 1.1 usually acts no better than about 1.5 in an environment with a high tone. If one lives in a low-toned environment he can expect, eventually, to be low-toned. This is also true of marriage—one tends to match the tone level of one's marital partner.

This tone scale is also valid for groups. A business or a nation can be examined as to its various standard reactions and these can be plotted. This will give the survival potential of a business or a nation.

42   This chart can also be used in employing people or in choosing partners. It is an accurate index of what to expect and gives you a chance to predict what people will do before you have any great experience with them. Also, it gives you some clue as to what can happen to you in certain environments or around certain people, for they can drag you down or boost you high.

A more extensive copy of this chart appears in the major text, *Science of Survival,* by L. Ron Hubbard, obtainable at all Dianetic organization bookstores in the back of this book.

The Hubbard Chart
of Human Evaluation   43

Definitions for words footnoted in this chart may be found immediately following the last page of the chart.

		1 Behavior and Physiology	2 Medical Range	3 Emotion
Tone Scale	4.0	Excellent at projects, execution. Fast reaction time (relative to age).	Near accident-proof. No psychosomatic ills. Nearly immune[1] to bacteria.	Eagerness, exhilaration.
	3.5	Good at projects, execution, sports.	Highly resistant to common infections. No colds.	Strong interest.
	3.0	Capable of fair amount of action, sports.	Resistant to infection and disease. Few psychosomatic ills.	Mild interest. Content.
	2.5	Relatively inactive, but capable of action.	Occasionally ill. Susceptible[2] to usual diseases.	Indifference. Boredom.
	2.0	Capable of destructive and minor constructive action.	Severe sporadic[3] illnesses.	Expressed resentment.
	1.5	Capable of destructive action.	Depository[4] illnesses (arthritis). (Range 1.0 to 2.0 interchangeable.)	Anger.
	1.1	Capable of minor execution.	Endocrine[5] and neurological[6] illnesses.	Unexpressed resentment. Fear.
	0.5	Capable of relatively uncontrolled action.	Chronic malfunction of organs. (Accident prone.)	Grief. Apathy.
	0.1	Alive as an organism.	Chronically ill. (Refusing sustenance.[7])	Deepest apathy.

4 Sexual Behavior ___ Attitude toward Children	5 Command over Environment	6 Actual Worth to Society Compared to Apparent Worth	
Sexual interest high but often sublimated[8] to creative thought. ___ Intense interest in children.	High self-mastery. Aggressive toward environ.[14] Dislikes to control people. High reasoning, volatile[15] emotions.	High worth. Apparent worth will be realized. Creative and constructive.	**4.0** Tone Scale
High interest in opposite sex. Constancy.[9] ___ Love of children.	Reasons well. Good control. Accepts ownership. Emotion free. Liberal.[16]	Good value to society. Adjusts environ to benefit of self and others.	**3.5**
Interest in procreation.[10] ___ Interest in children.	Controls bodily functions. Reasons well. Free emotion still inhibited. Allows rights to others. Democratic.[17]	Any apparent worth is actual worth. Fair value.	**3.0**
Disinterest in procreation. ___ Vague tolerance of children.	In control of function and some reasoning powers. Does not desire much ownership.	Capable of constructive action; seldom much quantity. Small value. "Well adjusted."	**2.5**
Disgust at sex; revulsion. ___ Nagging of and nervousness about children.	Antagonistic and destructive to self, others, and environ. Desires command in order to injure.	Dangerous. Any apparent worth wiped out by potentials of injury to others.	**2.0**
Rape. Sex as punishment. ___ Brutal treatment of children.	Smashes or destroys others or environ. Failing this, may destroy self. Fascistic.	Insincere. Heavy liability. Possible murderer. Even when intentions avowedly[20] good will bring about destruction.	**1.5**
Promiscuity,[11] perversion, sadism,[12] irregular practices. ___ Use of children for sadistic purposes.	No control of reason or emotions, but apparent organic control. Uses sly means of controlling others, especially hypnotism.[18] Communistic.[19]	Active liability. Enturbulates[21] others. Apparent worth outweighed by vicious hidden intents.	**1.1**
Impotency,[13] anxiety, possible efforts to reproduce. ___ Anxiety about children.	Barest functional control of self only.	Liability to society. Possible suicide. Utterly careless of others.	**0.5**
No effort to procreate.	No command of self, others, environ. Suicide.	High liability, needing care and efforts of others without making any contribution.	**0.1**

45

		7 Ethic Level	8 Handling of Truth	9 Courage Level
Tone Scale	4.0	Bases ethics on reason. Very high ethic level.	High concept of truth.	High courage level.
	3.5	Heeds ethics of group but refines them higher as reason demands.	Truthful.	Courage displayed on reasonable risks.
	3.0	Follows ethics in which trained as honestly as possible. Moral.[22]	Cautious of asserting truths. Social lies.	Conservative display of courage where risk is small.
	2.5	Treats ethics insincerely. Not particularly honest or dishonest.	Insincere. Careless of facts.	Neither courage nor cowardice. Neglect of danger.
	2.0	Below this point: authoritarian.[23] Chronically and bluntly dishonest when occasion arises.	Truth twisted to suit antagonism.	Reactive, unreasoning thrusts at danger.
	1.5	Below this point: criminal. Immoral. Actively dishonest. Destructive of any and all ethics.	Blatant[25] and destructive lying.	Unreasonable bravery, usually damaging to self.
	1.1	Sex criminal. Negative ethics. Deviously dishonest without reason. Pseudoethical[24] activities screen perversion of ethics.	Ingenious and vicious perversions of truth. Covers lying artfully.[26]	Occasional underhanded displays of action, otherwise cowardly.
	0.5	Nonexistent. Not thinking. Obeying anyone.	Details[27] facts with no concept of their reality.	Complete cowardice.
	0.1	None.	No reaction.	No reaction.

10 Speech: Talks Speech: Listens	11 Subject's Handling of Written or Spoken Comm[32] When Acting as a Relay Point	12 Reality[35] (Agreement)	Tone Scale
Strong, able, swift and full exchange of beliefs and ideas.	Passes theta comm, contributes to it. Cuts entheta[33] lines.	Search for different viewpoints in order to broaden own reality. Changes reality.	4.0
Will talk of deep-seated beliefs and ideas. Will accept deep-seated beliefs, ideas; consider them.	Passes theta comm. Resents and hits back at entheta lines.	Ability to understand and evaluate reality of others and to change viewpoint. Agreeable.	3.5
Tentative[28] expression of limited number of personal ideas. Receives ideas and beliefs if cautiously stated.	Passes comm. Conservative. Inclines toward moderate construction and creation.	Awareness of possible validity of different reality. Conservative agreement.	3.0
Casual pointless conversation. Listens only to ordinary affairs.	Cancels any comm of higher or lower tone. Devaluates[34] urgencies.	Refusal to match two realities. Indifference to conflict in reality. Too careless to agree or disagree.	2.5
Talks in threats. Invalidates[29] other people. Listens to threats. Openly mocks theta[30] talk.	Deals in hostile or threatening comm. Lets only small amount of theta go through.	Verbal doubt. Defense of own reality. Attempts to undermine others. Disagrees.	2.0
Talks of death, destruction, hate only. Listens only to death and destruction. Wrecks theta lines.	Perverts comm to entheta regardless of original content. Stops theta comm. Passes entheta and perverts it.	Destruction of opposing reality. "You're wrong." Disagrees with reality of others.	1.5
Talks apparent theta, but intent vicious. Listens little; mostly to cabal,[31] gossip, lies.	Relays only malicious comm. Cuts comm lines. Won't relay.	Doubt of own reality. Insecurity. Doubt of opposing reality.	1.1
Talks very little and only in apathetic tones. Listens little: mostly to apathy or pity.	Takes little heed of comm. Does not relay.	Shame, anxiety, strong doubt of own reality. Easily has reality of others forced on him.	0.5
Does not talk. Does not listen.	Does not relay. Unaware of comm.	Complete withdrawal from conflicting reality. No reality.	0.1

47

		13 Ability to Handle Responsibility	14 Persistence on a Given Course	15 Literalness of Reception of Statements
Tone Scale	4.0	Inherent sense of responsibility on all dynamics.[36]	High creative persistence.	High differentiation.[40] Good understanding of all comm, as modified by Clear's[41] education.
	3.5	Capable of assuming and carrying on responsibilities.	Good persistence and direction toward constructive goals.	Good grasp of statements. Good sense of humor.[42]
	3.0	Handles responsibility in a slipshod fashion.	Fair persistence if obstacles not too great.	Good differentiation of meaning of statements.
	2.5	Too careless. Not trustworthy.	Idle, poor concentration.	Accepts very little, literally or otherwise. Apt to be literal about humor.
	2.0	Uses responsibility to further own ends.	Persistence toward destruction of enemies. No constructive persistence below this point.	Accepts remarks of tone 2.0 literally.
	1.5	Assumes responsibility in order to destroy.	Destructive persistence begins strongly, weakens quickly.	Accepts alarming remarks literally. Brutal sense of humor.
	1.1	Incapable, capricious,[37] irresponsible.	Vacillation[38] on any course. Very poor concentration. Flighty.[39]	Lack of acceptance of any remarks. Tendency to accept all literally avoided by forced humor.
	0.5	None.	Sporadic persistence toward self-destruction.	Literal acceptance of any remark matching tone.
	0.1	None.	None.	Complete literal acceptance.

48

16 Method Used by Subject to Handle Others	17 Hypnotic Level	18 Ability to Experience Present-Time[45] Pleasure		
Gains support by creative enthusiasm and vitality backed by reason.	Impossible to hypnotize without drugs.	Finds existence very full of pleasure.	4.0	Tone Scale
Gains support by creative reasoning and vitality.	Difficult to trance[43] unless still possessed of a trance engram.	Finds life pleasurable most of the time.	3.5	
Invites support by practical reasoning and social graces.	Could be hypnotized, but alert when awake.	Experiences pleasure some of the time.	3.0	
Careless of support from others.	Can be a hypnotic subject, but mostly alert.	Experiences moments of pleasure. Low intensity.	2.5	
Nags and bluntly criticises to demand compliance with wishes.	Negates somewhat, but can be hypnotized.	Occasionally experiences some pleasure in extraordinary moments.	2.0	
Uses threats, punishment and alarming lies to dominate others.	Negates heavily against remarks, but absorbs them.	Seldom experiences any pleasure.	1.5	
Nullifies others to get them to level where they can be used. Devious and vicious means. Hypnotism, gossip. Seeks hidden control.	In a permanent light trance, but negates.	Most gaiety forced. Real pleasure out of reach.	1.1	
Enturbulates others to control them. Cries for pity. Wild lying to gain sympathy.	Very hypnotic. Any remark made may be a "positive suggestion."[44]	None.	0.5	
Pretends death so others will not think him dangerous and will go away.	Is equivalent to a hypnotized subject when "awake."	None.	0.1	

49

		19 **Your Value as a Friend**	**20** **How Much Others Like You**	**21** **State of Your Possessions**
Tone Scale	**4.0**	Excellent.	Loved by many.	In excellent condition.
	3.5	Very good.	Well loved.	In good condition.
	3.0	Good.	Respected by most.	Fairly good.
	2.5	Fair.	Liked by a few.	Shows some neglect.
	2.0	Poor.	Rarely liked.	Very neglected.
	1.5	Definite liability.	Openly disliked by most.	Often broken. Bad repair.
	1.1	Dangerous liability.	Generally despised.	Poor. In poor condition.
	0.5	Very great liability.	Not liked. Only pitied by some.	In very bad condition generally.
	0.1	Total liability.	Not regarded.	No realization of possession.

22 How Well Are You Understood	23 Potential Success	24 Potential Survival	
Very well.	Excellent.	Excellent. Considerable longevity.	**4.0** **Tone** **Scale**
Well.	Very good.	Very good.	**3.5**
Usually.	Good.	Good.	**3.0**
Sometimes misunderstood.	Fair.	Fair.	**2.5**
Often misunderstood.	Poor.	Poor.	**2.0**
Continually misunderstood.	Usually a failure.	Early demise.[46]	**1.5**
No real understanding.	Nearly always fails.	Brief.	**1.1**
Not at all understood.	Utter failure.	Demise soon.	**0.5**
Ignored.	No effort. Complete failure.	Almost dead.	**0.1**

Footnotes

1. immune: protected from a disease or the like.
2. susceptible: easily influenced by or affected with.
3. sporadic: 1. happening from time to time; not constant or regular; occasional.
4. depository: having to do with matter collected in any part of any organism.
5. endocrine: (of a gland) pouring its secretions straight into the blood, not through a duct.
6. neurology: the medical science of the nervous system and its disorders.
7. sustenance: 2. the food itself, nourishment.
8. sublimate: 1. to divert the energy of (an emotion or impulse arising from a primitive instinct) into a culturally higher activity.
9. constancy: 2. faithfulness.
10. procreate: to bring (a living thing) into existence by the natural process of reproduction, to generate.
11. promiscuity: 2. having sexual relations with many people.
12. sadism: 1. sexual gratification gained through causing physical pain or humiliation.
13. impotence: 2. complete failure or serious impairment of sexual power, especially in the male.
14. environ: surrounding area; vicinity.
15. volatile: 2. (of a person) lively, changing quickly or easily from one mood or interest to another.
16. liberal: 6. favoring or permitting freedom of action, especially with respect to matters of personal belief or expression.
17. democratic: 2. in accordance with the principle of equal rights for all.
18. hypnotism: amnesia trance for the purpose of planting suggestions.
19. communist: 1. an advocate of communism (2. a system of social organization in which all economic and social activity is controlled by a totalitarian state dominated by a single and self-perpetuating political party).
20. avow: to admit, to declare openly.
21. enturbulate: cause to be turbulent or agitated and disturbed.
22. moral: simply, totally and only—of or concerned with the judgment of the goodness or badness of human action and character; pertaining to good and evil. Designed to teach goodness or correctness of character and behavior; instructive of what is good and bad.
23. authoritarian: favoring complete obedience to authority as opposed to individual freedom.
24. pseudo-: (prefix) false, insincere.
25. blatant: very bad, obvious.
26. artful: 1. crafty; cunning; tricky.
27. detail: 1. to give particulars of, to describe fully.
28. tentative: hesitant, not definite, done as a trial.
29. invalidate: invalidation (refuting or degrading or discrediting or denying something someone else considers to be fact).
30. theta: reason, serenity, stability, happiness, cheerful emotion, persistence and other factors which man ordinarily considers desirable.
31. cabal: 1. a secret plot.
32. comm: abbreviation of communication.
33. entheta: means enturbulated theta (thought or life); especially refers to communications, which, based on lies and confusions, are slanderous, choppy or destructive in an attempt to overwhelm or suppress a person or group.
34. devaluate: 1. to deprive of value; reduce the value of.
35. reality: is fundamentally agreement. That which we agree to be real is real.

36. dynamics: in Dianetics, survival is understood to be the basic single thrust of life through time and space, energy and matter. Survival is subdivided into eight dynamics. Man does not survive for self alone, nor yet for sex, nor yet for groups, nor yet only for the species of man. Man apparently survives, as do other living organisms, along eight separate channels. These channels are called the dynamics.

37. capricious: characterized by or subject to whim; impulsive and unpredictable.

38. vacillate: 1. to waver in decision or opinion.

39. flighty: 1. given to sudden whims; not taking things seriously.

40. differentiate: 3. to perceive the difference in or between.

41. Clear: an unaberrated person. He is rational in that he forms the best possible solutions he can on the data he has and from his viewpoint. He obtains the maximum pleasure for the organism, present and future, as well as for the subjects along the other dynamics.

42. humor: humor is rejection. The ability to reject. The ability to throw something away. That is humor.

43. trance: 1. a half-conscious state, seemingly between sleeping and waking, in which ability to function voluntarily may be suspended. v. 6. to put in a trance.

44. positive suggestion: suggestion by the operator to a hypnotized subject with the sole end of creating a changed mental condition in the subject by implantation of the suggestion alone. It is a transplantation of something in the hypnotist's mind into the patient's mind. The patient is then to believe it and take it as part of himself.

53

45. present time: the ground, sky, walls, objects and people of the immediate environment. In other words, the anatomy of present time is the anatomy of the room or area in which you are at the moment when you view it.

46. demise: death.

54

CHAPTER EIGHT

Tone Scale Tests

Test Number One   55

Take this test before you begin on the Processing Section of *Self Analysis*.

Be fair and as honest as possible in your findings.

Use, as a basis, how you have been in the last year. Earlier conditions in your life do not count.

Open up chart to column 1, Behavior and Physiology. Ask yourself how active you are physically. Locate the place in this column which most nearly seems to fit you.

Look on the tone scale for the number of the square you have found. Is it 3.0? Is it 2.5?

Take this number and go to the graph at right.

Under column 1, as marked at the top of the graph, locate the number (3.0, 2.5 or whatever it was) and place an X in this square. This gives the same place on the graph that you found on the chart.

Go to column 2 on the chart, Medical Range.

Find the square which best describes your health. Note the number given in the tone scale column opposite the square you have chosen (3.5, 2.0 or whatever it was).

Turn back to the graph of Test One. In column 2 on the graph, put an X in column 2 opposite the tone scale number you got from the chart.

Carry through this process with all columns until you have an X in each column of the graph. Omit the last six.

Take a straight edge or ruler. Move it on the graph, holding it horizontally, until you have the level of the graph which contains the most X's. Draw a line through these X's all the way across the chart and out to the edge. This line will give you your position in the last six columns.

The horizontal line you have just drawn gives you your position on the tone scale. This level of the chart is yours.

Leave this graph in the book. Keep it so that you can compare it in a few weeks when you do Test Two.

Note that in columns 4 and 10 the squares are divided in the same manner as the squares on the chart. You make two evaluations of yourself for these columns and you put an X in a half square, using two half squares for each column, even if one X falls at 3.0 and the other X falls at 1.1.

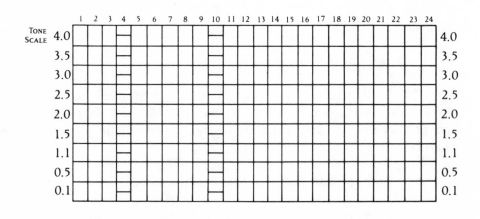

Test Number Two

Take this test after you have been processing yourself about two weeks, or about fifteen hours.

Use as your data how you have felt about things since taking Test One.

57

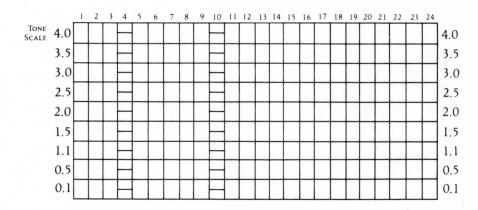

Test Number Three

Use this test after you have been processing yourself two months.

Use as data how you have felt about things since taking the second test.

Use the same directions as given in Test One.

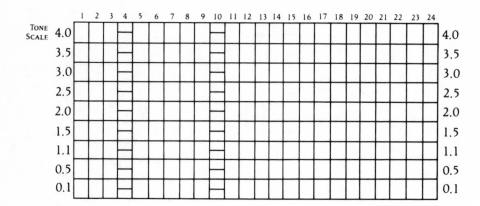

CHAPTER NINE

How to Use the Disc

A slotted disc is provided for the reader's use. The disc   59
must be used. Without using the disc, the benefit of processing is cut
more than eighty percent.

The disc is placed over question 1 of a list so that the
question shows through. One recalls[1] the incident[2] desired.

Then one looks at the upright word on the disc itself. This
says, for instance, *sight*.

One seeks to *see* in recall the incident desired.

One tries then to recall another incident without moving
the disc. He then seeks to *see* this incident in recalling it.

One tries to recall, then, the earliest incident of this kind
he can and seeks to *see* this one.

Then one drops the disc one question, rotating it at the
same time so that another sense appears upright. He uses this sense
particularly in recalling the incident.

Turn the disc over on each new page, so that a new set of
perceptions comes up.

It does not matter what sense you begin to recall with. It
does not matter which side you first begin to use.

---

1.   recall: present-time remembering something that happened in the past. It is not reexperiencing it, reliving it or rerunning it. Recall does not mean going back to when it happened. It simply means that you are in present time, thinking of, remembering, putting your attention on something that happened in the past—all done from present time.

2.   incident: an experience, simple or complex, related by the same subject, location, perception or people that takes place in a short and finite time period such as minutes, hours or days; also, mental image pictures of such experiences.

Eventually you should be able to get more and more perceptions on any one incident until, at last, you may recover all of them without strain.

If you lose the disc, the full list of perceptions on it are at the side of every page. Take a pencil and check them off one at a time just as though they were appearing on the disc.

A green disc and a white disc are provided. Use the one you like best.

60

If you only get a vague concept of what the sense must have been like, if you do not at first get actual recall by the sense itself, be sure that you at least get a conception of it.   □

Dianetic Processing

Dianetic Processing may be divided into two classes.

The first is Light Processing. This includes analytical[1] recall of conscious moments. It is intended to raise tone and increase perception and memory. It often resolves chronic somatics[2] (psychosomatic ills).

The second is Deep Processing. This addresses basic cause and locates and reduces moments of physical pain and sorrow. It is done without drugs or hypnosis by an auditor. Auditors have either learned Dianetics after a thorough study of the basic text *Dianetics: The Modern Science of Mental Health* or they have been trained professionally. Professional auditors can be contacted at any of the organizations listed in the back of this book.

61

This book contains Light Processing. This book is not "self-auditing." "Self-auditing" is nearly impossible. In this book, the author, L. Ron Hubbard, is actually giving the reader Light Processing. □

---

1.   analytical: capable of resolving, such as problems, situations. The word analytical is from the Greek análysis meaning resolve, undo, loosen, which is to say take something to pieces to see what it is made of. This is one of those examples of the shortcomings of the English language since no dictionary gives the word analytical any connection with thinking, reasoning, perceiving, which in essence is what it would have to mean, even in English.

2.   somatic: body sensation, illness or pain or discomfort. Soma means body. Hence psychosomatic or pains stemming from the mind.

62

CHAPTER TEN

Processing Section

Here begin the lists of questions by which the individual can explore his past and improve his reactions toward life. Dianetically speaking, this self-processing section could be called "Straightwire."[1] It is not "auto-processing." The reader is actually being processed by the author.

In the full use of Dianetics these questions could be considered as preparatory to co-auditing. The auditor is assisted by these lists in that they open a case[2] for the running of engrams and secondaries[3] and raise the preclear[4] on a tone scale. These question sections, so far as is known at this time, will not run out engrams and secondaries as such but will desensitize[5] them to a marked extent with a consequent improvement in the mental and physical being of the individual.

An auditor, as the practitioner in Dianetics is called since he both listens and computes, can use these questions during a session with a preclear. Further, two people can work with these sections—one of them asking the questions of another who answers—or both of them reading the questions and both of them attempting to get a recall on such an incident as that one called for.

These lists are used repetitively; that is to say the individual goes over them again and again. There is no finite period

63

---

1. Straightwire: the earliest coining of the memory exercises known as "Straightwire" came from the formula of cause and effect. We describe this as the act of stringing a line between present time and some incident in the past, and stringing that line directly and without any detours.
2. case opening: in starting a case we can say that we are trying to free all possible attention units (a theta energy quantity of awareness existing in the mind in varying quantity from person to person) as fast as possible.
3. secondary: a mental image picture of a moment of severe and shocking loss or threat of loss which contains unpleasant emotion such as anger, fear, grief, apathy or "deathfulness."
4. preclear: any person who has been entered into Dianetic processing.
5. desensitize: to make less sensitive to a substance or influence.

to the work. The reason the recall of these questions is important is that they reveal and discharge locks[6] which have formed above the basic[7] engrams and secondaries. The discharging of these locks renders engrams and secondaries relatively ineffective. A full Dianetic clearing[8] of the individual's engrams and secondaries gives the highest possible attainable results, but these questions provide self-processing which prepares the case for such an action and are in themselves highly beneficial.

64

In the process of using these questions the preclear may discover many manifestations in himself. He may experience considerable emotional release. He may become angry at the recollection of some of the things which have happened to him and he may even feel like crying over some of the losses he has sustained[9] and indeed may very well cry. However, the intent of these questions is not to focus the self-processor's attention upon the bad things which have happened to him but upon the good things which have taken place in his life. A concentration upon these happier circumstances tends to discharge the unhappy circumstances and render them far less forceful.

These questions are based upon the Dianetic discoveries, axioms[10] and postulates which have done so much toward amplifying the understanding of people, concerning the nature of existence and their roles in it. Life can be considered to have as its fundamental purpose survival in the material universe. When one closely examines survival he discovers that the concept embraces all the activities of an individual, a group, a state, life itself or the material universe.

The material universe is composed of matter, energy, space and time. Life can then be considered to be engaged upon the conquest of matter, energy, space and time, including other life forms, organisms and persons. If an organism or a group has been successful in handling other organisms, groups and the material universe, its survival potential is very great. If the organism has been unsuccessful,

---

6.   lock: a mental image picture of an incident where one was knowingly or unknowingly reminded of a secondary or engram. It does not contain unconsciousness. It may contain a feeling of pain or illness, etc., but is not itself the source of it.

7.   basic: the first experience recorded in mental image pictures of that type of pain, sensation, discomfort, etc. Basic is simply earliest.

8.   clearing: what is clearing but regaining awareness that one is himself and regaining confidence.

9.   sustain: 6. to undergo or suffer (an injury, loss, etc.).

10.   axioms: statements of natural laws on the order of those of the physical sciences.

its survival potential is lower. Its moments of success, as its moments of pain, are highly charged.[11] It is possible, by certain processes, to remove the charge from painful incidents. One of the ways of doing this is to lay the stress and concentration of the organism upon the times it has been successful in surviving.

With the invention of language man brought upon himself an unexpected source of aberration. While language itself is very far from the whole reason an organism is less successful than it might be, our current social order lays undue stress upon language. Words are only symbols which represent actions. A child learns these actions very early and learns the symbols which represent the actions. Later on he begins to mistake the action for the symbol and begins to believe the words themselves have force and power which they do not. If you believe that words have force and power, hold your hand in front of your mouth and say a few words. You will see how negligible is the force of utterance, no matter what words you use. Underlying this mistaken emphasis on the force of words lie actual physical actions of which the words are the symbols. The main point then is that words are not powerful but actions are. For example, when an individual has been told to hold still he obeys simply because he has experienced earlier in his life the action of being made to hold still by physical force.

65

For many reasons it is important for the organism to increase its mobility. The discovery of all the times the organism has been told to hold still and has obeyed has some therapeutic value but the discovery of actual incidents when the organism has been physically forced to remain motionless is much more important in restoring the mobility of the organism.

These lists, then, tend to devaluate the importance of language. This is only one of their many functions but an important one; therefore, the reading of these lists should direct the individual to moments action took place, not when somebody said it took place. Just as hearsay evidence[12] is not admissible in a court of law, so are words and phrases given to the individual by others inadmissible in self-processing. For instance, when one is asked for a time when somebody went away one should not try to recall the time when

---

11. charge: stored energy or stored re-creatable potentials of energy.
12. hearsay evidence: testimony given by a witness based on what he has heard from another person.

somebody said somebody went away or the statement that somebody was going away, but the actual physical departure, regardless of what was said.

You will find that words are communicated through the physical universe to other organisms. Sounds, for instance, originate within the organism, are translated into sound waves and reach the other person as sound waves. The written word is made into symbols of ink, which are then seen, the other physical fact of light, by another organism. Whereas there may very well be such things as ESP,[13] it is not aberrative.

66

There are many perceptions, which is to say channels, through which one can contact the physical universe. You are aware of the physical universe because of sight, sound, mouth and other message systems. Therefore, each time you are asked to recall an incident of a certain kind you will be asked, after you have recalled it, to pay attention to a certain sense channel which was present during the time when you experienced the incident. The circular disc is provided for this purpose. You will notice the disc has two sides. The perceptions or sense messages listed on one side are different from those on the other side. As you read the questions one after the other you should read them through a slot provided in this disc. Going to the next question you should rotate the slot once counterclockwise for each new question. This will give you a new perception. For instance the question may pertain[14] to a time somebody went away from you. You will recall a time when this occurred, selecting the moment of actual physical departure. Undoubtedly you will get some perception of the scene and you may even get a very full perception of the scene. Many people see, feel, hear and otherwise perceive memories when they recall them. Some people are too occluded.[15] These lists wipe away occlusion. As you recall the person walking away from you then, you are not supposed to recall merely the concept that somebody had walked away, but the moment when they actually did and get as many perceptions as possible of them doing so. The disc which overlies this question will have upright at random one particular perception. That perception may be *sound*—thus you should attempt to recover whatever sounds were present when this

---

13.   ESP: extrasensory perception: perception or communication outside of normal sensory activity, as in telepathy and clairvoyance.
14.   pertain: 3. to have reference or relevance; be related.
15.   occluded: memory not available for recall. Someone who is occluded has a poor memory and poor recalls of the past.

individual walked away as the particular emphasis of perception. *If you are unable to recover the sounds as such, hearing them again, at least recover the concept of what they may have been.*

If you will examine this disc, you will find that it lists six perceptions with which you have contacted the physical universe. Actually there are many more of these than six.

When the word *emotion* is upright above a question after you have recalled the incident suggested by the question, you then try to recall in particular and feel again, if possible, the emotion you felt at the time. When the next question is addressed the disc is rotated one turn counterclockwise. You will find that *loudness* is now upright. You should get an incident in recall suggested by the question and having perceived the incident you should then give your attention in particular to the loudness of the various sounds in the incident.

67

Going to the next question, you should rotate the disc once more counterclockwise. You will find that *body position* is now upright. You should read the question and recall some incident it suggests, perceive it as well as you possibly can and then give particular attention to the position your own body was in at the time the incident occurred. Going to the next question and rotating the disc once more you will find that *sound* is now upright. You should recall the incident the question calls for and then give particular attention to the sounds in that incident. Going to the next question and rotating the disc once more, you will find that *weight* is upright. In the incident you recall you should then give attention to the heaviness of things, including the pull of gravity on yourself and the weight of anything you may actually be supporting in the incident such as your clothes, a ball or any other thing which you are actually holding at the time the incident occurred.

Rotating the disc once more to the next question on the list, you will find that *personal motion* falls upright. When you have answered the question then you should give attention to the motion which you yourself were undertaking at the time the incident occurred.

Every time you go to a new page you should turn the disc upside down. You will find here a new set of perceptics.[16] These, of course, are applied in such a way that when you go over the list a second time you will probably not have the same perception, as these things fall at random. Thus while you might have answered a question the first time about somebody coming toward you with attention to sound called for by the disc, the next time you reach this question, on going over the list again, you may find *emotion* upright. You should then contact any and all emotion on the second time, whereas you contacted the sound the first time. You will find on the reverse side of the disc the perceptions of *sight, smell, touch, color, tone* and *external motion*. *Sight* is what you actually saw at the time. A person whose perceptions are in good condition will see again what he has seen before when the incident actually occurred. Thus *sight* calls for what was seen while the incident called for was taking place. *Smell* requests the individual to recall any and all odors which were present during the scene he is recalling. *Touch* requests the recall of anything the individual was actually touching at the time with the sensation of touch, including pressure. One is always in contact with the material world in terms of touch, even if only the touch of his feet on the ground or the feel of his clothes upon him. The perception of *color,* when upright, should cause the individual to try to perceive again the color which was contained in the scene called for. When *tone* is requested the individual should attempt to contact the quality of the sound present when the scene occurred. When *external motion* is upright, the individual, in recalling the incident called for by the question, should attempt to perceive in the incident recalled the movement contained in the incident, the motion of other people or objects or of energy.

As one goes over these questions then with the disc, he is exploring his own life and during that exploration is attempting to call into view with the highest possible level of reality those things he has perceived. The immediate result is a heightening of perception of his present-time world. Another result is a strengthening of his memory. Yet another result is the rearrangement and reevaluation of things which have happened to him. Another and more mechanical and fundamental result is the deintensification of unpleasant experiences—like bringing them into the light. For a while one may feel it is better to forget unpleasant things. Forgotten, they have more force and destructive quality than when examined.

68

---

16.   perceptics: any sense messages such as sight, sound, smell, etc.

The individual will find himself, as he repeatedly uses a list, getting earlier and earlier incidents. It is not impossible for him to remember straight back to the earliest beginnings of his life, much less his infancy.

Again, and it cannot be emphasized too strongly, these questions are requesting actual physical actions, not statements about physical actions. It is perfectly legitimate to recall scenes which have been seen in the movies or read about in books, but when one recalls such scenes one should have full awareness, in the case of the movies, of the screen and the seat and where the incident is taking place and when. In the case of books one should get not the scene the author would like the reader to see but the actual scene of reading and the recall should be recaptured in terms of print and sitting in a chair, not in terms of imagining.

69

There is a great deal of technology out of sight back of these questions. All that is important is that this operation, continued persistently, going over one list and then another and recalling the things required, considerably improves the individual's thinking and acting abilities and his physical well-being and considerably enhances his relationship with his present environment.

You will find the very last list is named the "End of Session List." This means that after you have worked a list, or worked as long as you desire to, during any one period of self-processing, you should turn to the "End of Session List" and answer the questions as a routine operation.

You will also find a list entitled "When Uncomfortable," which is placed next to the last in the book. If you find during a session of self-processing that you grow considerably uncomfortable or unhappy, you should then turn to the "When Uncomfortable" list. Using it should restore your good spirit swiftly.

If you find it is extremely difficult to recall any one question in these lists, simply pass over it and go to the next question. If you find you are having difficulty in answering any of these lists you will do better if some friend reads them to you.

If undergoing self-processing makes you extremely unhappy it is probable that your case should be given the attention of a Dianetic auditor until such time as you are capable of handling this matter for yourself.

You can go over a list many times before going on to the next list or you can continue on through all of the lists consecutively without repeating any. You will probably find that going over each list many times before going on to the next will work better than going through the book consecutively. You will notice that after you have been over the same memory several times, even though it be an unpleasant one, that it will cease to have any effect upon you. This means its intensity is decreasing and that the energy which it contained and which was affecting your present-time life is dissipating.[17] If you can remember several incidents of the same kind, do so; and if they are troublesome to you, simply go over the things you remembered once more, one after the other, and then again. This, Dianetically speaking, is called Repetitive Straightwire.[18] It deintensifies unpleasant memories. However, this list is aimed toward the recall of pleasant incidents. Pleasant incidents do not deintensify as unpleasant ones do but, underneath the level of attention, deintensify unpleasant incidents when the pleasant incident is recalled.

All you really need to work these lists is to know that actions, not words, are required and that the disc should be used to give you the particular kind of recall you should have on the recollection called for. If you lose the disc you will note that the side of the page has a list of the perceptions for your reference. When using the side-of-the-page list you should merely take the recalls, the perceptions, consecutively one after the other and use them the same way you used them with the disc.

Don't simply answer questions yes or no. Select an actual moment in your life called for by the question. Try to resense that moment with the perceptic called for on the disc.

If going over the questions makes you unhappy, simply continue with the list you are working, over and over. The unhappiness should "wear out" after unhappy incidents are recalled many times. The feeling will turn to one of relief.

---

17.   dissipate: 1. to break up and scatter; dispel; disperse.
18.   Repetitive Straightwire: Straightwire to one incident done over and over until the incident is desensitized.

Some people are frightened at the idea of persevering with these questions. Certainly you've got more nerve than that. The worst they could do is kill you.

Don't be surprised if you feel sleepy after using some of these questions. The sleepiness is only a symptom of relaxing. The very least this book can do for you is replace your sedatives![19]

If, while answering these questions, you begin to yawn, that is good. Yawning is a release of former periods of unconsciousness. You may yawn so much the tears come out of your eyes. That is progress.

71

Should you feel very groggy while answering these questions, that is only "boil-off," the manifestation of former periods of unconsciousness boiling off. Simply persist in recalling the incident or others like it and the feeling will pass away, leaving you more alert than before. If you interrupt this "boil-off" and stop your session, you may feel cross or irritable. This grogginess occasionally amounts to nearly complete unconsciousness, but it always goes away. That unconsciousness was what was keeping you from being high on the tone scale.

Occasionally vague or even sharp pains may turn on and off as you are answering questions. Don't try to find out where they came from. They will go away if you persist with these questions. Simply ignore them. They are the ghosts of what they used to call psychosomatic ills, former injuries restimulated.[20]

An individual is suppressed by these deposits of past pain and unconsciousness. Self Analysis makes such past moments pass away and deintensify at least partially, without your having to find out what was in them.

A full description of these manifestations and their causes occurs in Science of Survival, the popular text on Dianetics, which you will find on the book list in the back of this book.

---

19. sedative: a drug that allays (calms, puts to rest) irritability, nervousness or excitement.
20. restimulate: the reactivation of a past memory due to similar circumstances in the present approximating circumstances of the past.

Important
*Use lists many times. Try for the earliest
incident you can get for each question.*

72

General Incidents

The purpose of this list is to give you practice in 73 recalling things. Use the disc provided in the front of the book and look at the beginning of this section for instructions as to how this list is to be used.

Can you recall a time when:

☐ *Sight*
☐ *Smell*
☐ *Touch*
☐ *Color*
☐ *Tone*
☐ *External Motion*
☐ *Emotion*
☐ *Loudness*
☐ *Body Position*
☐ *Sound*
☐ *Weight*
☐ *Personal Motion*

1. You were happy.

2. You had just finished constructing something.

3. Life was cheerful.

4. Somebody had given you something.

5. You ate something good.

6. You had a friend.

7. You felt energetic.

8. Somebody was waiting for you.

9. You drove fast.

10. You saw something you liked.

11. You acquired something good.

74

□ *Sight*
□ *Smell*
□ *Touch*
□ *Color*
□ *Tone*
□ *External Motion*
□ *Emotion*
□ *Loudness*
□ *Body Position*
□ *Sound*
□ *Weight*
□ *Personal Motion*

12. You threw away something bad.

13. You kissed somebody you liked.

14. You laughed at a joke.

15. You received money.

16. You felt young.

17. You liked life.

18. You played a game.

19. You bested[1] something dangerous.

20. You acquired an animal.

21. Somebody thought you were important.

22. You chased something bad.

23. You were enthusiastic.

24. You owned something.

25. You enjoyed life.

26. You went fast.

27. You enjoyed a good loaf.

28. You felt strong.

29. Somebody you disliked departed.

30. Somebody helped you.

31. You gathered something good.

32. You measured something.

---

1.   best: to defeat, to outdo, to outwit.

33. You took a pleasant journey.

34. You turned on a light.

35. You heard some good music.

36. You controlled something.

37. You destroyed something.

38. You mastered something.   75

□ Sight
□ Smell
□ Touch   39. You were lucky.
□ Color
□ Tone   40. You felt peaceful.
□ External
   Motion   41. You saw a pretty scene.
□ Emotion
□ Loudness   42. You poured something good.
□ Body
   Position   43. You acquired something that was
□ Sound   scarce.
□ Weight
□ Personal   44. You made an enemy scream.
   Motion
              45. You had a pleasant seat.

46. You handled something well. (actual
    physical handling)

47. You moved something.

48. You watched something fast.

49. You were together with friends.

50. You occupied a good space.

51. Somebody loved you.

52. You enjoyed somebody.

53. You invented something.

54. You harnessed some energy.

55. You killed a bug.

56. You pocketed something.

57. You made progress.

58. You walked.

76

□ *Sight*
□ *Smell*
□ *Touch*
□ *Color*
□ *Tone*
□ *External Motion*
□ *Emotion*
□ *Loudness*
□ *Body Position*
□ *Sound*
□ *Weight*
□ *Personal Motion*

59. You saved something.

60. You stopped a machine.

61. You started a machine.

62. You had a good sleep.

63. You stopped a thief.

64. You stood under something.

65. You started a fire.

66. You went upstairs.

67. You were warm.

68. You went riding.

69. You were adroit.[2]

70. You swam.

71. You stood your ground.

72. You lived well.

73. You were respected.

74. You won a race.

75. You ate well.

---

2.   adroit: skillful, ingenious.

Time Orientation

This list is intended to aid your general sense of time 77 as applied to periods in your life. Everyone has a full recording of everything that happened to him during his life. It may be that he cannot immediately recall certain periods. These periods are said to be occluded. Working with these lists in general, such occluded periods will gradually disappear when one's life is in recall, to the betterment of his mental and physical well-being and his perception of his present-time environment. In Dianetics it is considered that everyone has a "time track."[1] Everything which an individual has perceived throughout his life is recorded on this "time track" from the beginning to the end. It is dangerous to have occlusions since the data in the occluded area becomes compulsive and causes less than optimum conduct. This list is intended to straighten out the track in general. Do not be dismayed if you cannot recall the actual instant of the memory. Get the memory first. If you can answer the remaining questions, that is all to the good.

Can you recall an incident which happened:

1. A long time ago. (the year? the month? the date? the hour?)

2. Yesterday. (the hour? the date?)

3. Last month. (position of the sun?)

4. When you were very small. (clothes people wore? position of sun?)

---

1.   time track: consists of all the consecutive moments of "now" from the earliest moment of life of the organism to present time.

5. When you were half your present size. (the sizes of others at that time?)

6. When you were a third your present weight. (position of the sun?)

7. When your mother looked younger. (her clothes? position of the sun?)

8. When you felt agile.[2] (the year? the hour?)

9. Last Christmas. (time of day?)

10. Your fifth Christmas. (clothing of others?)

11. Your eighth birthday. (furniture?)

12. A birthday. (the appearance of others? year? position of sun?)

13. This day last year. (the house you lived in? the date? the season?)

14. At noon today.

15. At a banquet. (clothing of people present?)

16. At a marriage. (year? season?)

17. At a birth. (season?)

18. On a date with someone. (hairdo?)

19. About a clock. (position of the sun?)

20. About a wrist watch. (motion of second hand?)

78

□ Sight
□ Smell
□ Touch
□ Color
□ Tone
□ External Motion
□ Emotion
□ Loudness
□ Body Position
□ Sound
□ Weight
□ Personal Motion

---

2. agile: nimble, quick-moving.

21. With an animal. (when it was smaller?)

Can you recall incidents which compare:

1. Clothing today and clothing when you were small.

☐ Sight
☐ Smell
☐ Touch
☐ Color
☐ Tone
☐ External Motion
☐ Emotion
☐ Loudness
☐ Body Position
☐ Sound
☐ Weight
☐ Personal Motion

79

2. Hairdo today and hairdo when you were in your teens.

3. Something which is now old when it was new.

4. Something which was small which is now big.

5. Something which is now old when it was young.

6. The way the sun shines in the morning and in the afternoon.

7. Winter with summer.

8. Spring with winter.

9. Fall with spring.

10. Sunrise with sunset.

11. A morning shadow and an evening shadow.

12. Clothing now old when it was new.

13. A house now standing where no house was.

14. An open space which is now cut up.

15. A long time and a short time.

16. A cigarette when it was lighted and when it was put out.

17. The beginning and the end of a race.

18. Bedtime and getting up.

80

□ Sight
□ Smell
□ Touch
□ Color
□ Tone
□ External Motion
□ Emotion
□ Loudness
□ Body Position
□ Sound
□ Weight
□ Personal Motion

19. School in the morning and getting out in the afternoon.

20. Your size now and when you were little.

21. A cloudy day and a sunshiny day.

22. Stormy weather and rainy weather.

23. Something hot and when it got cold.

24. Something young and something old.

25. A fast heartbeat and a slow heartbeat.

26. When you were overheated and when you were chilly.

27. When you had lots of room and when you had little room.

28. When the light was bright and when it was dim.

29. When a fire burned bright and when it died down.

30. An object half-built and when it was started.

31. The same person when he was big with when he was small.

32. When you felt little and when you felt grown up.

33. Yesterday morning with this morning.

34. A complete calendar and when it had its leaves torn off.

☐ Sight

☐ Smell

☐ Touch

35. A stopped clock and a running clock.

☐ Color

☐ Tone

36. The sun's motion and the moon's motion.

☐ External
   Motion

☐ Emotion

☐ Loudness

37. When you felt tired and when you felt energetic.

☐ Body
   Position

☐ Sound

38. Cars then with cars now.

☐ Weight

☐ Personal
   Motion

39. When you started this list and this question.

82

Orientation
of Senses

This list is arranged especially to call your attention   83
to the existence of many of the channels by which you perceive
yourself and the physical universe about you. While each of the
questions listed pertains to a specific sense channel such as sight
or sound, the disc could still be used, for what is required are specific
moments when you were using various senses and any specific
moment includes many other sense messages than the one which is
called for. Therefore, use the disc as in any other questions, and after
you have recalled a specific incident called for in the question then
try recalling it with specific attention to that sense which happens to
be upright on the disc at that time.

Time Sense

Anyone has a sense of time. This sense is apt to become
aberrated. The existence of clocks at every hand seems to tell us that
we need mechanical assistance in knowing what time it is. The first
person that had an aberrated or dearranged time sense made the first
clock desirable—but only for him. Clocks and calendars are artificial
symbols representing time which is an actual commodity and which
can be sensed directly by the individual. This section and almost
every other section in these lists rehabilitates the sense of time. Time
in most people's minds is confused with space. The words which
describe time are also the words which describe space, which shows
that man has an indifferent attention for his time sense. The organism measures time in many ways, but mostly in terms of motion
and growth or decay. Change is the most striking symbol of time
passage, but there is a direct sense of time which everyone has
although it may be occluded by a society which, using clocks and
calendars, seems to invalidate the fact that it exists. You should have
no confusion of any kind about time.

Can you recall a time when:

84

- □ *Sight*
- □ *Smell*
- □ *Touch*
- □ *Color*
- □ *Tone*
- □ *External Motion*
- □ *Emotion*
- □ *Loudness*
- □ *Body Position*
- □ *Sound*
- □ *Weight*
- □ *Personal Motion*

1. It was very late.

2. You were early.

3. You had to wait.

4. You had to stand for some time supporting a weight.

5. You went very fast.

6. You covered a great deal of space.

7. You used a lot of time (when you really did, not when somebody said you did).

8. An object ran down (not a clock).

9. A long length of space.

10. A short length of space.

11. An object moving.

12. An animal moving.

13. A clock hand moving.

14. A round object.

15. An object near an object.

16. A lightning bolt.

17. Breaking a watch. (did time stop?)

18. A good time.

19. You were too late.

20. Somebody lived too long.

Additional time questions are in the second half of List Two.

Sight

There are several portions of the sense channel called sight. Light waves, coming from the sun, moon, stars or artificial sources, reflect from objects and the light waves enter the eyes and are recorded for present-time action or as memory for future reference. Light sources are also recorded. This is the sense perception called *sight*. It has subdivisions. First of these might be considered to be motion, wherein sight depends upon a time span to record a continuously changing picture. While one may see motion in present time, various aberrations of sight may cause him to recall only still pictures. Nevertheless, all the motions are still recorded and can be recalled as moving pictures. In this way all other senses have a dependence upon time in order to bring in the message of motion, since motion is also recorded by the other perceptions. More particularly, part of sight is color perception. There are people who are color blind in present time; that is to say, they can see color but are unable to perceive differences of shading. There are people who may see color in present time but in trying to recall what they have seen, recall only in black and white. This would be recall color blindness. The color is fully deleted. It is an aberration easily remedied when one recalls things he has seen in color as black and white or as still pictures.

Another part of sight is *depth perception*. Depth perception is observed in two ways. One is by seeing the difference in size of objects and so having a conception of the fact that one is further back than another or that the object itself is at a distance and the other is a "stereoscopic"[1] effect occasioned[2] by the fact that one has two eyes.

---

1.   stereoscopic: giving a three-dimensional effect.
2.   occasion: to cause.

Each eye sees a little bit around the object and so true depth perception is possible. Still one may have two eyes and not have depth perception in present-time observation. Additionally, one may see perfectly well with depth perception in present time and yet, in recall, see pictures flat and without depth perception. This lack of depth perception is again remediable. An individual who could not perceive motion in present time and who additionally could not perceive color or depth would be a very bad risk as a driver; almost as bad is that individual who cannot recall what he has seen; or if he can recall it, cannot do so with depth perception, full color and motion. This part of this list is devoted to giving you a better insight into sight. All these perceptics are exercised over and over by these lists in general. If you cannot immediately see in recall what you have looked at some other time simply try to get a concept of how things looked at specific times.

Can you recall a sight which was:

☐ *Sight*
☐ *Smell*
☐ *Touch*
☐ *Color*
☐ *Tone*
☐ *External*
   Motion
☐ *Emotion*
☐ *Loudness*
☐ *Body*
   Position
☐ *Sound*
☐ *Weight*
☐ *Personal*
   Motion

1. Very bright.

2. Dark.

3. Green.

4. Vast.

5. Moving.

6. Flat.

7. Deep.

8. Colorful.

9. Swift.

10. Slow.

11. Pleasant.

12. Desirable.

13. Pretty.

14. Rare.

15. Remarkable.

16. Confused.

17. Mysterious.

☐ *Sight*
☐ *Smell*
☐ *Touch*
☐ *Color*
☐ *Tone*
☐ *External Motion*
☐ *Emotion*
☐ *Loudness*
☐ *Body Position*
☐ *Sound*
☐ *Weight*
☐ *Personal Motion*

18. Lazy.

19. Warm.

20. Cheerful.

21. Nearly invisible.

22. Blurred.

23. Sharply defined.

24. Lovable.

25. Passionate.

26. Joyful.

27. Very real.

28. Something you can really recall well with sight.

Relative Sizes

The recognition of one's size in relationship to the scene in which he finds himself and the objects and organisms of that scene is, in itself, a sense message. It is particularly trying on children and undoubtedly was on you when you were a child, to be surrounded with objects which were so large. When one is actually getting a good recall on a childhood incident he is quite often startled to see how big things appeared to him and how large were those giants, the adults, with which he was surrounded. The feeling of being small in the vicinity of large objects sometimes produces the feeling of inadequacy. It is even said that people who are smaller than the average feel less secure in their environment. This evidently stems from the fact that their grown-up size has not reached the average and thus the feeling of smallness and inadequacy during childhood is in constant restimulation. It is not because the person, though smaller, is really inadequate. In such a way people who are taller than the average become aware of the fact, mostly because people smaller than themselves find ways and means of nullifying them because of their size. The perception of relative size is therefore an important perception to rehabilitate and a person who is larger than others on the average would do well to change the reading disc with which he is working these questions so that the word *loudness* on the disc is marked out and *relative size* is substituted.

88

Can you recall a time when:

☐ *Sight*
☐ *Smell*
☐ *Touch*
☐ *Color*
☐ *Tone*
☐ *External Motion*
☐ *Emotion*
☐ *Loudness*
☐ *Body Position*
☐ *Sound*
☐ *Weight*
☐ *Personal Motion*

1. You were bigger than an animal.

2. You were smaller than an object.

3. You were bigger than a person.

4. You were smaller than a person.

5. Things looked little to you.

6. Things looked big to you.

7. You were in a vast space.

8. You looked at the stars.

9. You were dwarfed by an object.

10. You saw a giant.

11. Somebody waited on you.

12. You scared somebody.

13. You chased somebody.

14. You licked a larger boy.

15. Furniture was too small for you.

16. A bed was too small for you.

17. A bed was too big for you.   89

☐ Sight
☐ Smell
18. A hat didn't fit.
☐ Touch
☐ Color
19. You had to be polite.
☐ Tone
☐ External
   Motion
20. You bullied somebody.
☐ Emotion
☐ Loudness
21. Your clothes were too large.
☐ Body
   Position
22. Your clothes were too small.
☐ Sound
☐ Weight
23. The vehicle was too large.
☐ Personal
   Motion
24. The vehicle was too small.

25. A space was too big.

26. A table was too big.

27. Your arm was too big.

28. A cook was small.

29. You could reach something above you.

30. A ball was too small.

31. A daughter was smaller.

32. A desk was too small.

Can you recall:

33. A big fork.

34. A small kettle.

35. A small hill.

36. A small fish.

90

☐ Sight
☐ Smell
☐ Touch
☐ Color
☐ Tone
☐ External Motion
☐ Emotion
☐ Loudness
☐ Body Position
☐ Sound
☐ Weight
☐ Personal Motion

37. A little flower.

38. A small doctor.

39. A tiny dog.

40. A small man.

41. A little child.

42. A small cat.

43. A little house.

44. A small machine.

45. Short legs.

46. A small face.

47. A small place.

Sound

Sound consists of the perception of waves emanating from moving objects. An object moves rapidly or slowly, and sets into vibration the air in its vicinity which pulses. When these pulses strike the eardrum they set into motion the individual's sound-recording mechanism and the sound is registered. Sound is absent in a vacuum[1]

---

1.   vacuum: 1. a space with nothing at all in it; completely empty space.

and is actually merely a force wave. Sound in too great a volume or too discordant[2] can be physically painful, just as light in too great a quantity can hurt the eyes. However, the amount of nervousness occasioned by sound, as by light, is mainly an aberration and it is not warranted,[3] since the sound itself is not ordinarily damaging, and there are few incidents in anyone's life when a sound has had enough physical force to be physically damaging. Apprehension[4] and anxiety about the physical universe and other persons can, however, cause the individual to be nervous about sound, as it is one of the most reliable warning mechanisms; but starting at every sound in a civilized environment, being afraid of voices of others, or even traffic noises, is foolish, since men rarely live a tooth-and-claw existence which warrants such attention. As sound becomes intermingled with past pain, the individual mistakes the moment and time he is hearing the sound, and so may associate it, as he may with other perceptics, with past pain. These lists permit an individual to rehabilitate his skill in telling the difference between one time and another or one situation and another.

91

Sound has several parts. The first is pitch. This is the number of vibrations per unit of time of any object from which sound is coming. The second is quality or tone, which is simply the difference between a jagged or ragged sound wave and a smooth sound wave as in a musical note. The third is volume, which merely means the force of the sound wave, its loudness or quietness.

Rhythm is actually a part of the time sense, but is also the ability to tell the spaces between sound waves which are pulsing regularly, as in the beating of a drum.

Many people have what is called extended hearing, which is to say they have too high an alertness to sounds. This accompanies, quite ordinarily, a general fear of the environment or the people in it. There is also deafness by which the individual simply shuts out sounds. Some deafness is, of course, occasioned by entirely mechanical trouble with the recording mechanism, but most deafness, particularly when partial, is psychosomatic, or caused by mental aberration. The individual may or may not be able, at first, to

---

2.   discordant: 2. disagreeable to the ear; harsh.
3.   warrant: 2. to serve as justification or reasonable grounds for (an act, belief, etc.).
4.   apprehension: 1. a feeling of fear about a possible danger or difficulty.

recall what he has heard and which has been recorded in the past, when he remembers it. In other words, he does not get a sound when he remembers that he heard a sound. This is an occlusion of sound recordings. Recalling a sound by hearing it again is called sonic in Dianetics and is a desirable circumstance which can be returned to the individual.

It is interesting to note that there is also a depth perception in sound. A person having two ears gets a "stereoscopic" effect on sources of sound so that he can tell how far they are from him and where they are located in relationship to him.

92

Can you recall a time when you heard:

□ Sight
□ Smell
□ Touch
□ Color
□ Tone
□ External Motion
□ Emotion
□ Loudness
□ Body Position
□ Sound
□ Weight
□ Personal Motion

1. A gentle wind.

2. A quiet voice.

3. A pleasant sound.

4. A pleasant voice.

5. A breeze.

6. A dog whining.

7. A bell.

8. A cheerful voice.

9. A musical instrument.

10. A door close.

11. Water running.

12. Liquid coming from a bottle.

13. Good food frying.

14. A ball rolling.

15. A wheel singing.[5]

16. A car starting.

17. A child laughing.

18. A ball bouncing.

☐ Sight
☐ Smell
☐ Touch
☐ Color
☐ Tone
☐ External
   Motion
☐ Emotion
☐ Loudness
☐ Body
   Position
☐ Sound
☐ Weight
☐ Personal
   Motion

19. A sewing machine running.   93

20. A cat mewing.

21. A pen writing.

22. A child running.

23. A book page turning.

24. A newspaper being opened.

25. A kiss.

26. A stimulating sound.

27. A smooth sound.

28. A rhythmic sound.

29. A happy sound.

30. A rubbing sound.

31. An enthusiastic sound.

32. A sigh.

33. An eager voice.

34. A revelry.[6]

---

5.   sing: 2. to make a shrill whining or whistling sound.
6.   revelry: boisterous (rough and noisy) festivity.

35. A band.

36. A silky sound.

37. Restful water.

38. A sound in a big place.

39. A wanted sound.

40. An endearing[7] sound.

41. A domestic sound.

42. A busy sound.

43. A pleasant noise.

44. A far-off sound.

45. A nearby sound.

46. A number of sounds jumbled together.

47. A safe sound.

48. A sound that is very real to you.

□ Sight
□ Smell
□ Touch
□ Color
□ Tone
□ External Motion
□ Emotion
□ Loudness
□ Body Position
□ Sound
□ Weight
□ Personal Motion

94

Olfactory[1]

The sense of smell is evidently activated by small particles escaping from the object, which is thus sensed traveling through space and meeting the nerves. When one comes to think of it, this seems rather unpleasant at times, but there are also many very pleasant smells.

---

7.   endearing: 2. expressing affection.

1.   olfactory: 1. of or pertaining to the sense of smell.

The sense of smell has four subdivisions which are mainly categories of the type of odor.

Taste is usually considered to be a part of the sense of smell.

Can you recall a time when you smelled the following:

☐ Sight
☐ Smell
☐ Touch
☐ Color
☐ Tone
☐ External Motion
☐ Emotion
☐ Loudness
☐ Body Position
☐ Sound
☐ Weight
☐ Personal Motion

95

1. Something sweet.

2. Something sharp.

3. Something oily.

4. Something pungent.[2]

5. Something desirable.

6. Something burned.

7. Something stimulating.

8. Something cheerful.

9. A good person.

10. A happy person.

11. A warm person.

12. A friendly animal.

13. A pleasant leaf.

14. Cut grass.

15. Something passionate.[3]

---

2. pungent: 1. having a strong sharp taste or smell.
3. passionate: 3. resulting from, expressing, or tending to arouse strong feeling; intense.

16. Something you wanted.

17. Something you threw away.

18. A bird.

19. Something exciting.

20. Something desirable.

96

☐ *Sight*
☐ *Smell*
☐ *Touch*
☐ *Color*
☐ *Tone*
☐ *External Motion*
☐ *Emotion*
☐ *Loudness*
☐ *Body Position*
☐ *Sound*
☐ *Weight*
☐ *Personal Motion*

21. A child.

22. Face powder.

23. Perfume.

24. Lipstick.

25. Leather.

26. Pipe smoke.

27. Sweat.

28. Wool.

29. Clean sheets.

30. Fresh air.

31. A bouquet.

32. Money.

33. Paper.

34. Furniture.

35. A beautiful morning.

36. A party.

37. A pleasant odor that is very real to you.

Can you recall a time when you tasted the following:

1. Soup.

2. Eggs.

☐ *Sight*
☐ *Smell*
☐ *Touch*
☐ *Color*
☐ *Tone*
☐ *External Motion*
☐ *Emotion*
☐ *Loudness*
☐ *Body Position*
☐ *Sound*
☐ *Weight*
☐ *Personal Motion*

3. Bread.

4. Biscuits.

5. Coffee.

6. Tea.

7. Milk.

8. Cereal.

9. Dumplings.

10. Fish.

11. Beef.

12. Chicken.

13. A steak.

14. Duck.

15. Stuffing.

16. Cheese.

17. A fillet.[4]

97

---

4.   fillet: 6. a boneless, lean piece of meat or fish.

18. Potatoes.

19. Watermelon.

20. A cocktail.

21. Liquor.

22. A hot sandwich.

98

☐ *Sight*
☐ *Smell*
☐ *Touch*
☐ *Color*
☐ *Tone*
☐ *External Motion*
☐ *Emotion*
☐ *Loudness*
☐ *Body Position*
☐ *Sound*
☐ *Weight*
☐ *Personal Motion*

23. Jelly.

24. Ice cream.

25. Pudding.

26. Candy.

27. Pickles.

28. Punch.

29. A vegetable.

30. An apple.

31. An orange.

32. A fruit.

33. Cake.

34. Something you really thought was well cooked.

35. Something you like to eat raw.

36. A cookie.

37. A cracker.

38. Meat.

39. Something cold.

40. Something warm.

41. Your favorite dish.

42. Something in a swanky⁵ place.

43. Something at a party.

☐ *Sight*
☐ *Smell*
☐ *Touch*
☐ *Color*
☐ *Tone*
☐ *External Motion*
☐ *Emotion*
☐ *Loudness*
☐ *Body Position*
☐ *Sound*
☐ *Weight*
☐ *Personal Motion*

44. Something in the open.

45. Something on a holiday.

46. Something when you were very hungry.

47. Something which was rare.

48. Something which made you feel good.

49. Something for which you were grateful.

50. Something you had waited for a long time.

51. Something you had not been able to get.

52. Something you stole.

99

Touch

The sense of touch is that communication channel which informs the central control system of the body whenever some portion of the body is in contact with the material universe, other organisms, or the organism itself. Probably the sense of touch is the oldest sense in the terms of the central nervous system.[1] It has four

---

5.   swanky: 1. elegant or smart.

1.   central nervous system: the brain and the spinal cord.

100

subdivisions. The first of these is pressure; the second is friction; the third is heat or cold; and the last is oiliness. Just as an individual can be hard of hearing or have bad eyesight, so can his sense of touch be dulled or even almost absent. This condition is known as anesthesia. Just as in any other perceptic, the sense of touch can be pleasurable, unpleasant or painful. When an individual has been considerably harmed, as in accidents, illness or injury, he tends to cut communication with the physical universe and other organisms, just as he cuts communication by getting bad eyesight, becoming hard of hearing, etc. Not only can the sense of touch be dulled in some people, but it can be too sensitive in others who have this sense channel aberrated until it seeks to contact danger more avidly[2] than danger exists. One of the manifestations of the aberrated sense of touch is too high a sensitivity to sexual contact, rendering it painful or anxious, or a dulling of this contact so that sensation can be nearly absent. A sense of touch is very important. It is partially responsible for pleasure, as in sex, and is to a large measure responsible for the sensation we know as physical pain. The sense of touch extends from the central nervous system to the skin surface and as such is intimately connected and most basically in contact with the physical universe. Sight and sound and the olfactory systems contact things usually at a distance, whereas touch is alert only to the closest proximity of actual contact. Touch is partially responsible for the pleasure taken in food and crosses, to this extent, the sense of taste. As a demonstration of how poorly the sense of touch serves many people, try laying your hand in a friendly fashion on the shoulder of someone. All too many people will dodge or shrink away from the contact. An aberrated sense of touch is partially responsible for a dislike of food as well as impotency and antipathy[3] for the sexual act. The rehabilitation of the sense of touch goes a long way toward rehabilitating one's confidence in one's environment and considerably enhances survival by making it possible for the individual to obtain pleasure, where before there might only have been distaste.

---

2.   avid: 2. eager and enthusiastic.
3.   antipathy: 1. a strong or deep-rooted dislike.

Can you recall an incident when you felt (touched):

1. The pressure on your feet while you stood.

2. A fork.

3. A greasy surface.

☐ Sight
☐ Smell
☐ Touch
☐ Color
☐ Tone
☐ External Motion
☐ Emotion
☐ Loudness
☐ Body Position
☐ Sound
☐ Weight
☐ Personal Motion

4. The pressure of a movie seat.   101

5. A steering wheel.

6. A cat.

7. Another person.

8. Cool clothing.

9. Your hair.

10. A child.

11. Something you admired.

12. Something new.

13. An arm.

14. A ball.

15. An easy chair.

16. A collar.

17. A poker.[4]

18. A musical instrument.

19. Something comfortable.

---

4.   poker: a stiff metal rod for poking a fire.

20. Something which gave you confidence.

21. Something bright.

22. A desk.

23. A girl.

24. A boy.

102

□ Sight
□ Smell
□ Touch
□ Color
□ Tone
□ External Motion
□ Emotion
□ Loudness
□ Body Position
□ Sound
□ Weight
□ Personal Motion

25. A fish.

26. A doll.

27. Silk.

28. Velvet.

29. Your ear.

30. Your body.

31. Something which made you feel enthusiastic.

32. Something which delighted you.

33. Something you desired eagerly.

34. Someone who was faithful.

35. A happy child.

36. A generous hand.

37. A good machine.

38. A pleasant letter.

39. A newspaper containing good news.

40. A telephone when you received good news.

41. A hat.

42. A dear[5] face.

43. A stair bannister.

44. A kind object.

103

□ Sight
□ Smell
□ Touch
□ Color
□ Tone
□ External Motion
□ Emotion
□ Loudness
□ Body Position
□ Sound
□ Weight
□ Personal Motion

45. A moving object.

46. An object you loved.

47. An enemy being hurt.

48. A polite person.

49. Something pretty.

50. Something which made you rejoice.

51. A food you liked.

52. Something you believed in.

53. Something you liked to stroke.

54. A strong person.

55. A little person.

56. Water you enjoyed.

57. A shower.

58. An old person.

59. Something warm.

60. Something cold.

---

5.   dear: 1. much loved; beloved.

□ *Sight*

□ *Smell*

□ *Touch*

□ *Color*

□ *Tone*

□ *External
  Motion*

□ *Emotion*

□ *Loudness*

□ *Body
  Position*

□ *Sound*

□ *Weight*

□ *Personal
  Motion*

104

61. A wind.

62. A sleepy person.

63. A cool bed on a warm night.

64. Something which made you enthusiastic.

65. Something you touched this morning.

66. Something you are touching now.

Personal Emotion

There are many emotions. The principal ones are happiness, boredom, antagonism, anger, covert hostility,[1] fear, grief and apathy. Other emotions are usually simply greater or lesser magnitude than the ones listed. Terror, for instance, is a volume of fear. Sadness is a small volume of grief. Dejection is a small part of apathy. Love is an intensity of happiness addressed in a certain direction. These emotions form a gradient scale which make up in Dianetics the emotion section of the tone scale. Happiness is the highest emotion and apathy is the lowest. A person can be chronically emotional along any level of this tone scale. An individual tends to move up or down this scale through these various listed emotions in the order of the first sentence.

Emotion monitors or regulates the endocrine system. The perceptions and the central nervous system call for certain emotional secretions to catalyze[2] the body to meet the various situations in the environment. Emotion is one of the easiest things to aberrate. There are individuals who feel they must be perpetually sad, even when their circumstances should make them happy. There are individuals

---

1.   covert hostility: here is the person who hates but is afraid to say he hates, who deals in
     treachery and who yet expects to be forgiven.
2.   catalyze: to act upon by catalysis (the causing or accelerating of a chemical change by the
     addition of a substance that is not permanently affected by the reaction).

who believe they have to be happy regardless of their environment and who yet are very miserable. Most people are not emotional—they are misemotional, in that they do not react to the situations in their environment with the emotion which would be most rational to display. The social order has confused irrationality[3] with emotionalism. Actually a person who is fully rational would be most able to respond to the stimulus of his environment. Being rational does not mean being cold and calculating. An individual who is rationally happy can be counted upon to make the best calculations. Without free emotion, an individual cannot appreciate as he should the pleasant things in his environment. Lack of appreciation for art or music comes about when the individual cannot be freely emotional. The person who feels he must be cold-blooded in order to be rational is what is called in Dianetics a "control case," and on examination will be found to be very far from as rational as he might be. People who cannot experience emotion because of their aberrations are ordinarily sick people. Well people can experience emotion.

Derangements in the endocrine system, such as the thyroid,[4] the pancreas[5] and other glands, come about because of aberrations concerning emotion. It has been conclusively tested and proven in Dianetics that function controls structure. To a man or a woman who is aberrated sexually, injections of hormones[6] are of little or no avail in moving the mental aberrations which make injections ineffective. Removing emotional aberration rehabilitates the endocrine system so that the injections are usually not even necessary. When a person's emotional reaction becomes frozen, he can expect various physical difficulties such as ulcers,[7] hypothyroid[8] conditions, diabetes[9] and other ills which are more or less directly traceable to the endocrine system.

---

3. irrationality: the inability to get right answers from data.

4. thyroid: a large ductless gland at the front of the neck, secreting a hormone that regulates the body's growth and development.

5. pancreas: a large, elongated gland situated behind the stomach and secreting a digestive juice into the small intestine: groups of . . . cells in the gland produce the hormone insulin (a protein hormone which helps the body use sugar and other carbohydrates).

6. hormone: 1. a substance formed in some organ of the body . . . [glands] and carried by a body fluid to another organ or tissue, where it has a specific effect: now often prepared synthetically.

7. ulcer: an open sore on the surface of the body or one of its organs.

8. hypothyroid: of, characterized by, or having hypothyroidism (1. deficient activity of the thyroid gland. 2. disorder resulting from this).

9. diabetes: a disease in which sugar and starch are not properly absorbed by the body.

Inhibited or excessive misemotionalism is one of the most destructive things which can occur in the human organism. A person who is so aberrated is unable to experience happiness and so enjoy life. His physical body will not thrive.

Can you recall an incident when:

106

□ *Sight*
□ *Smell*
□ *Touch*
□ *Color*
□ *Tone*
□ *External Motion*
□ *Emotion*
□ *Loudness*
□ *Body Position*
□ *Sound*
□ *Weight*
□ *Personal Motion*

1. Somebody was angry.

2. Somebody wanted something.

3. You desired something.

4. You were happy.

5. You were pleased.

6. You won by being antagonistic.

7. You felt affectionate.

8. You admired something.

9. Something was amiable.[10]

10. You were amused.

11. You approved of an object.

12. You were surprised by something pleasant.

13. You attacked something successfully.

14. You attacked someone.

15. You were "attached" to something.

16. You had to blush.

---

10.   amiable: feeling and inspiring friendliness, good-tempered.

17. You felt bold.

18. You couldn't be bothered.

19. You were energetic.

20. You found out you weren't clumsy.

21. You were satisfied.

☐ *Sight*
☐ *Smell*
☐ *Touch*
☐ *Color*
☐ *Tone*
☐ *External Motion*
☐ *Emotion*
☐ *Loudness*
☐ *Body Position*
☐ *Sound*
☐ *Weight*
☐ *Personal Motion*

22. You cared for somebody.   107

23. You were confident.

24. You influenced somebody.

25. You were glad to be idle.

26. Somebody was patient.

27. You enjoyed life.

28. You were joyful.

29. You laughed.

30. You were in love.

31. You received good news.

32. You enjoyed the music.

33. You thought it was pretty.

34. You were satiated.[11]

35. You were passionate.

36. You prevented something.

37. You produced something.

---

11.   satiate: 2. to satisfy to the full.

38. You were glad to avoid a quarrel.

39. You were glad to hurt somebody.

40. You rejoiced.

41. You felt very safe.

42. You screamed with laughter.

108

☐ *Sight*
☐ *Smell*
☐ *Touch*
☐ *Color*
☐ *Tone*
☐ *External Motion*
☐ *Emotion*
☐ *Loudness*
☐ *Body Position*
☐ *Sound*
☐ *Weight*
☐ *Personal Motion*

43. You enjoyed the silence.

44. You got to go to bed.

45. You found it was a beautiful day.

46. You won the struggle.

47. You subdued a person.

48. You conquered something.

49. You obtained what you wanted.

50. You surprised somebody.

51. You contributed.

52. You were permitted to handle something.

53. You were glad you didn't have to be sorry.

54. You found the anxiety was for nothing.

55. You discovered your suspicions were unfounded.[12]

56. You finally got rid of it.

---

12.   unfounded: 1. not founded on fact or truth; baseless.

57. You stopped somebody from being terrified.

58. You were happy.

59. Somebody understood you.

60. Somebody listened to you respectfully.

61. You felt energetic.

109

62. You were vigorous.

☐ Sight
☐ Smell
☐ Touch
☐ Color
☐ Tone
☐ External Motion
☐ Emotion
☐ Loudness
☐ Body Position
☐ Sound
☐ Weight
☐ Personal Motion

63. You knew it was well done.

64. You didn't have to wait any more.

65. You liked to watch.

66. You stopped somebody from weeping.

67. You wandered at will.

68. You felt free.

69. You helped somebody.

70. You felt young.

71. You won.

72. You were glad to be together.

73. You were glad to leave.

74. You liked emotion.

75. You enjoyed moving.

76. The motion gave you joy.

77. You caught sight of something you had been waiting for.

78. You received a present you liked.

79. You found something out.

80. You pushed something away.

81. You pulled something to you.

82. You produced something.

110

□ Sight
□ Smell
□ Touch
□ Color
□ Tone
□ External
Motion
□ Emotion
□ Loudness
□ Body
Position
□ Sound
□ Weight
□ Personal
Motion

83. You were proud of it.

84. You raised something high.

85. You prevailed.[13]

86. You harnessed some energy.

87. You made the time pleasant.

88. You were glad to be with a friend.

89. You made something obey.

90. You were happy to give offense.

91. You realized your luck was good.

92. You overcame antagonism.

93. You found it was fun to leap.

94. You got out of work.

95. You didn't have to sit there any more.

96. You realized it was the last day of school.

97. You were happy it was real.

98. You felt virtuous.

---

13.   prevail: 1. to be victorious, to gain the mastery.

99. You knew you had shown courage.

100. Your desire was gratified.

101. You succeeded in your deception.

102. You conquered dejection.

103. You were glad it was over.

Sight
Smell
Touch
Color
Tone
External Motion
Emotion
Loudness
Body Position
Sound
Weight
Personal Motion

104. You waited eagerly.   111

105. You dispersed¹⁴ them.

106. You could tell the difference.

107. Your parent was proud of you.

108. Somebody was faithful to you.

109. You escaped.

110. You found you had hidden without cause.

111. You frightened somebody.

112. You overcame conservatism.

113. You discovered a friend.

114. You were friendly.

115. You did something that was forbidden and got away with it.

116. You gave somebody the gate.¹⁵

117. You healed something.

118. You acquired a pet.

14.   disperse: to scatter, to go or drive or send in different directions.
15.   gate, give (someone) the: 12b. to dismiss from one's employ.

119. It was a relief.

120. You found you weren't hurt.

121. You received a pleasant call.

122. Your income was increased.

123. You found you had influence.

112

□ *Sight*
□ *Smell*
□ *Touch*
□ *Color*
□ *Tone*
□ *External Motion*
□ *Emotion*
□ *Loudness*
□ *Body Position*
□ *Sound*
□ *Weight*
□ *Personal Motion*

124. You were ambitious.

125. You succeeded.

126. You found you didn't want it after all.

127. You conquered being poor.

128. Many were proud of you.

129. You were loved.

130. They rejoiced for you.

131. You were considered remarkable.

132. You kept a secret.

133. Someone believed in you.

134. You understood.

135. You showed your skill.

136. They liked you.

137. Somebody was happy.

138. Someone appreciated you.

139. You felt you had done a good job.

140. A child loved you.

141. A friend needed you.

142. They laughed at your joke.

143. Everybody was surprised.

144. You were sought after.

145. You were invited.

☐ Sight
☐ Smell
☐ Touch
☐ Color
☐ Tone
☐ External Motion
☐ Emotion
☐ Loudness
☐ Body Position
☐ Sound
☐ Weight
☐ Personal Motion

146. Someone made you realize you were strong.

147. You were important.

148. You found yourself necessary.

149. It was worthwhile.

150. You knew you had given pleasure.

151. You were well.

152. Someone was delighted with you.

153. You won the struggle.

154. You were believed.

155. You rescued somebody.

156. You discovered you weren't weak.

157. They stopped fighting you.

158. Somebody became afraid of you.

159. You made somebody successful.

160. You dispersed anxiety.

161. You were looked up to.

113

162. Somebody was glad you were there.

163. You conquered sorrow.

164. You were glad they were watching.

165. You could go and come as you pleased.

166. They gave you a chair.

114

□ *Sight*
□ *Smell*
□ *Touch*
□ *Color*
□ *Tone*
□ *External Motion*
□ *Emotion*
□ *Loudness*
□ *Body Position*
□ *Sound*
□ *Weight*
□ *Personal Motion*

167. You were rewarded.

168. You decided for yourself.

169. You found you were right.

170. You enjoyed youth.

171. You yelled for happiness.

172. You received what you wanted.

173. They discovered you were valuable.

174. You gave great happiness.

175. You were glad you had done it.

176. You found you weren't vain[16] after all.

177. You avoided them successfully.

178. You became important.

179. You were no longer unhappy.

180. You got to go.

181. You conquered some energy.

182. You fixed it.

---

16.   vain: 1. conceited, especially about one's appearance.

183. They found you had been wrongly suspected.

184. Your understanding was swift.

185. You discovered you didn't have to be ashamed.

186. You succeeded in your struggle.

187. You were glad to shake hands.

188. You enjoyed the kiss.

189. It was good to run.

190. You were able to retain it.

191. You restored it.

192. You did not have to go to bed.

193. You averted[17] ruin.

194. You found a refuge.[18]

195. It was good not to have to regret it.

196. You were true to your purpose.

197. You had lots of time.

198. You got out.

199. Somebody was glad you wrote.

200. Your people appreciated you.

201. You grew up.

□ Sight
□ Smell
□ Touch
□ Color
□ Tone
□ External Motion
□ Emotion
□ Loudness
□ Body Position
□ Sound
□ Weight
□ Personal Motion

115

---

17.   avert: 2. to prevent, to ward off.
18.   refuge: 1. shelter or protection from danger, trouble, etc.

116

□ *Sight*
□ *Smell*
□ *Touch*
□ *Color*
□ *Tone*
□ *External Motion*
□ *Emotion*
□ *Loudness*
□ *Body Position*
□ *Sound*
□ *Weight*
□ *Personal Motion*

202. You could make all the noise you wanted.

203. It wasn't necessary to do anything.

204. You obliged[19] somebody.

205. It was a wonderful occasion.

206. You were glad you were in love.

207. You couldn't lose.

208. You got them enthusiastic.

209. You sold it.

210. They enjoyed your music.

211. You laughed last.

212. You found out you weren't lazy.

213. They discovered you weren't ignorant.

214. They wanted your influence.

215. You didn't have to hurry.

216. You illuminated something beautiful.

217. You did the impossible.

218. You didn't have to worry about income.

219. You saw somebody come in that you liked.

220. You saw somebody leave that you disliked.

---

19.   oblige: 2. to help or gratify by performing a small service.

221. You felt fit.

222. Your fears were groundless.

223. It was all right to be excited.

224. You felt equal to anything.

225. It was a brilliant morning.

□ Sight

226. Life was full of zest.

117

□ Smell

□ Touch

227. They let you have enough.

□ Color

□ Tone

228. The drink was welcome.

□ External
   Motion

229. You were glad to eat.

□ Emotion

□ Loudness

230. It was so good to hug someone.

□ Body
   Position

231. You delivered the goods.

□ Sound

□ Weight

232. You were depended upon.

□ Personal
   Motion

233. Nobody could deny you anything.

234. You found you hadn't been deceived.

235. You deserved it.

236. You crawled under the covers.

237. They let you continue.

238. You could be as contrary[20] as you
     wanted.

239. The doctor was wrong.

240. Somebody cooked for you.

241. You had a nice house.

20.   contrary: 4. inclined to oppose or disagree stubbornly; perverse.

242. You found it was a pretty country.

243. You discovered you didn't have to stay there.

244. You got a better title.

245. You found something valuable.

246. You could keep any company you wanted.

247. You discovered it wasn't too complicated.

248. They had confidence in you.

249. You helped them conquer something.

250. You could leave the classroom.

251. You didn't have to go there any more.

252. Somebody came when you called.

253. You enjoyed a new car.

254. You got out of the cage.

255. They admitted you were clever.

256. You found your hands were adroit.

257. You discovered you could run faster.

258. You discovered you didn't have to mind.

259. You found it wasn't in vain[21] after all.

260. Hope paid off.

118

☐ *Sight*
☐ *Smell*
☐ *Touch*
☐ *Color*
☐ *Tone*
☐ *External Motion*
☐ *Emotion*
☐ *Loudness*
☐ *Body Position*
☐ *Sound*
☐ *Weight*
☐ *Personal Motion*

---

21.   in vain: with no result, uselessly.

☐ *Sight*
☐ *Smell*
☐ *Touch*
☐ *Color*
☐ *Tone*
☐ *External Motion*
☐ *Emotion*
☐ *Loudness*
☐ *Body Position*
☐ *Sound*
☐ *Weight*
☐ *Personal Motion*

261. You had a right to think for yourself.

262. You found you didn't have to be disappointed.

263. You discovered how persistent you were.

264. You knew you could handle responsibility.

265. The world was all yours.

266. You were delighted.

267. You felt good this morning.

119

Organic Sensation

Organic sensation is that sense which tells the central nervous system the state of the various organs of the body. Don't be alarmed if you feel groggy for a while or if you yawn prodigiously.[1] These manifestations are good and they will pass away if you recall a certain additional number of recollections on the same question that made you feel strange.

Can you recall a time when:

1. You felt yourself to be in good physical condition.

2. You enjoyed yourself physically.

3. You had just eaten something you liked.

4. Your head felt good.

---

1.   prodigious: 2. enormous.

5. Your back felt good.

6. You felt very relieved.

7. You were excited.

8. You felt very much alive.

9. You were proud of your body.

120

☐ *Sight*
☐ *Smell*
☐ *Touch*
☐ *Color*
☐ *Tone*
☐ *External Motion*
☐ *Emotion*
☐ *Loudness*
☐ *Body Position*
☐ *Sound*
☐ *Weight*
☐ *Personal Motion*

10. Your body was competent.

11. Your heart was beating calmly.

12. You didn't have a single ache or pain.

13. You felt refreshed.

14. Everybody was having a good time.

15. Both of you enjoyed it.

16. Your back felt strong.

17. You stood very straight.

18. You liked your position.

19. You got a new position.

20. You needed and got a cool drink of water.

21. Your head felt clear.

22. It was good to breathe fresh air.

23. You got it up.

24. You got it out.

25. You felt strong again.

26. You had eaten a good dinner.

27. You were enjoying it.

28. You did it with ease.

29. You poured something out.

30. You were tense with excitement.

☐ Sight

31. You were relaxed.   121

☐ Smell

☐ Touch

32. Your chest felt good.

☐ Color

☐ Tone

33. Your throat felt good.

☐ External
    Motion

34. Your eyes felt good.

☐ Emotion

☐ Loudness

35. You weren't aware of your breathing.

☐ Body
    Position

36. Your ears weren't ringing.

☐ Sound

☐ Weight

37. Your hands did something competent.

☐ Personal
    Motion

38. Your legs served you well.

39. Your feet felt good.

40. You knew you looked good.

Motion Personal

Amongst the various perceptions is that of personal motion. This is awareness of change of position in space. Many other perceptions assist this awareness of motion of self. This perception is assisted by sight, the feel of wind, changes in body weight and by the observation of external environment. However, it is a perceptic in itself and in the following questions your attention is called simply to the internal awareness of yourself in motion.

122

Can you recall a time when:

□ Sight
□ Smell
□ Touch
□ Color
□ Tone
□ External
　Motion
□ Emotion
□ Loudness
□ Body
　Position
□ Sound
□ Weight
□ Personal
　Motion

1. You were running.

2. You were walking.

3. You enjoyed a stroll.

4. You overcame something.

5. You threw something away you didn't want.

6. You won a tug of war.

7. You skipped rope.

8. You rode.

9. You did something successful in sports.

10. You lay down.

11. You stood up.

12. You turned around and around.

13. You jumped.

14. You stood on something that moved.

15. You leaped up.

16. You won a race.

17. You did something you were admired for physically.

18. You enjoyed moving.

19. You enjoyed standing still.

☐ *Sight*

☐ *Smell*

☐ *Touch*

☐ *Color*

☐ *Tone*

☐ *External Motion*

☐ *Emotion*

☐ *Loudness*

☐ *Body Position*

☐ *Sound*

☐ *Weight*

☐ *Personal Motion*

20. You pointed out something.

21. You showed yourself superior physically.

22. Your right hand did something skillful.

23. Your left hand did something skillful.

24. You tamed an animal.

25. You bested another person.

26. You did something physical you enjoyed.

27. You stepped up.

28. You held something close to you.

29. You threw something away you didn't want.

30. You felt lazy.

31. You turned the page of a book you enjoyed reading.

32. You dressed.

33. You got up when you wanted to.

34. You enjoyed wrestling with somebody.

35. You handled a complicated object successfully.

36. You drove well.

37. You carried some weight.

124

☐ Sight
☐ Smell
☐ Touch
☐ Color
☐ Tone
☐ External Motion
☐ Emotion
☐ Loudness
☐ Body Position
☐ Sound
☐ Weight
☐ Personal Motion

38. You gathered things together.

39. You packed.

40. You wouldn't let something go.

41. You enjoyed the morning.

42. You danced well.

43. You amused people because you wanted to.

44. You refused to do what was wanted of you and did what you wanted.

45. You were glad you were you.

46. You were complimented on posture.

47. You shook hands with somebody you were glad to see.

48. You grabbed something you desired.

49. You combed your hair.

50. You picked up this book.

51. You sat down a little while ago.

Motion External

The observation of external motion is accomplished by many sense channels. The ability to perceive motion in present time and the ability to recall things which have moved and perceive that they are moving are two different things. Inability to perceive well various motions occurring in one's environment is dangerous, but it is caused by the misapprehension[1] that the movements one perceives are dangerous when they most ordinarily are not. For every dangerous motion in one's environment there are countless thousands of safe and friendly motions. Because motion has been dangerous in the past is no reason to conceive[2] all motion as dangerous. Possibly one of the most aberrative actions above the level of unconsciousness is striking a person suddenly when he does not expect it. Slapping children, particularly when they are not alert to the fact that they are about to be slapped, tends to give an individual a distrust of all motion and even when they become of an age when a slap would be the last thing they would expect they still continue to distrust motion. In recalling motions you have seen externally, make an effort to see the actual movements which were around you.

125

Can you recall a time when:

☐ Sight
☐ Smell
☐ Touch
☐ Color
☐ Tone
☐ External Motion
☐ Emotion
☐ Loudness
☐ Body Position
☐ Sound
☐ Weight
☐ Personal Motion

1. Something pleasant moved very fast.

2. You saw somebody you didn't like running away from you.

3. You enjoyed seeing the rain come down.

4. You enjoyed seeing children play.

5. Trees rustled in a summer wind.

6. A quiet brook flowed.

7. You played ball.

---

1.   misapprehend: to misunderstand.
2.   conceive: 3. to hold as an opinion; think; believe.

8. You saw a kite flying.

9. You were exhilarated riding downhill.

10. You saw a bird fly gracefully.

11. You perceived the moon had moved.

12. You scared an animal away from you.

126

□ Sight
□ Smell
□ Touch
□ Color
□ Tone
□ External
  Motion
□ Emotion
□ Loudness
□ Body
  Position
□ Sound
□ Weight
□ Personal
  Motion

13. You saw a graceful dancer.

14. You saw an accomplished musician.

15. You saw an excellent actor.

16. You watched a graceful girl.

17. You watched a happy child.

18. You started an object.

19. You stopped an object.

20. You broke something you didn't like.

21. You watched a graceful man.

22. You enjoyed watching a ferocious animal.

23. You were glad to see something fall.

24. You watched something going around and around.

25. You enjoyed bouncing something.

26. You were happy to see something shoot up in the air.

27. You watched a fast horse.

28. You heard something swift.

29. You saw a "shooting star."

30. You saw grass moving in the wind.

31. You watched the second hand of a clock.

32. You saw somebody you didn't like walk away from you.

33. You saw somebody you liked walk toward you.

34. Somebody ran up and greeted you.

35. You saw an animal chasing an animal.

36. You moved an object.

37. You lifted an object.

38. You threw an object down.

39. You watched a friendly fire.

40. You saw a light come on.

41. You saw something go into something.

42. You emptied something.

43. You pulled something out.

44. You heard a friendly movement.

45. You destroyed something you didn't want.

46. You turned the page of this book.

☐ Sight
☐ Smell
☐ Touch
☐ Color
☐ Tone
☐ External Motion
☐ Emotion
☐ Loudness
☐ Body Position
☐ Sound
☐ Weight
☐ Personal Motion

Body Position

One is aware of the position of one's body by special perceptions. These include joint position. With the following questions give particular attention in the incident you recall to the position of your body at the time the incident occurred.

Can you recall a time when:

128

□ *Sight*
□ *Smell*
□ *Touch*
□ *Color*
□ *Tone*
□ *External Motion*
□ *Emotion*
□ *Loudness*
□ *Body Position*
□ *Sound*
□ *Weight*
□ *Personal Motion*

1. You enjoyed just sitting.

2. You fought your way out of a place you didn't want to be.

3. You stood and enjoyed a view.

4. You put your toe in your mouth.

5. You tried to stand on your head.

6. You tried to see if you could be a contortionist.[1]

7. You drank something pleasant.

8. You ate an excellent meal.

9. You drove a good car.

10. You were doing something you liked.

11. You enjoyed handling something.

12. You were competent in a sport.

13. You were admired.

14. You were happy.

---

1. contortionist: a performer who can twist his body into unusual postures.

15. You enjoyed a chance to sit down.

16. You enthusiastically stood up to go someplace.

17. You got rid of something.

18. You watched a child being trained.

19. You wanted to stay and did.

20. You wanted to leave and did.

129

☐ Sight
☐ Smell
☐ Touch
☐ Color
☐ Tone
☐ External Motion
☐ Emotion
☐ Loudness
☐ Body Position
☐ Sound
☐ Weight
☐ Personal Motion

130

Standard Processing

One can consider that the missions of the energy   131
of life, or at least one of them, is the creation, conservation,[1] main-
tenance, acquisition, destruction, change, occupation, grouping and
dispersal of matter, energy, space and time, which are the component
factors of the material universe.

So long as an individual maintains his own belief in his
ability to handle the physical universe and organisms about him and
to control them if necessary or to work in harmony with them, and
to make himself competent over and among the physical universe
of his environment, he remains healthy, stable and balanced and
cheerful. It is only after he discovers his inabilities in handling
organisms, matter, energy, space and time, and when these things
have been sharply painful to him, that he begins to decline physically,
become less competent mentally, and to fail in life. These questions
are aimed toward the rehabilitation of his ability to handle organisms
and the physical universe.

It was a pre-Dianetic error that an individual was healthy
so long as he was adjusted to his environment. Nothing could be less
workable than this "adaptive" postulate and had anyone cared to
compare it with actuality he would have discovered that the success
of man depends upon his ability to master and change his environment. Man succeeds because he adjusts his environment to
him, not by adjusting himself to the environment. The "adjusted"
postulate is indeed a viciously dangerous one, since it seeks to
indoctrinate the individual into the belief that he must be a slave to
his environment. The philosophy is dangerous because the people so
indoctrinated can be enslaved in that last of all graveyards, a welfare

---

1.   conservation: 1. the act of conserving; preservation from loss, injury, decay or waste.

state. However, this postulate is very handy in case one wishes to subjugate[2] or nullify human beings for his own ends. The effort in the direction of adjusting men to their environment by giving them "social training," by punishing them if they are bad, and by otherwise attempting to subdue and break them, has filled the society's prisons and insane asylums to the bursting point. Had anyone cared to look at the real universe he would have found this to be true: No living organism can be broken by force into an adjusted state and still remain able and amiable. Any horse trainer, for instance, knows that the horse must not be pushed or broken into submission if one wishes to retain his abilities, but, as they used to say in the army, mules were far more expensive than men, and perhaps it was not in the interest of pre-Dianetic thought to preserve men in a happy state. However, one should not be too harsh on these previous schools of thought since they had no knowledge of the natural laws of thought and in the absence of these, criminals can only be punished and not cured and the insane can only be driven down into the last dregs[3] of tractability.[4] The nearer to death, according to those schools of thought, the better, as witness electric shock "therapy"[5] and brain surgery—those efforts on the part of the mental medical men to as closely approximate euthanasia as possible without crossing the border into the legal fact of death. These past schools have now been taken under the wing of Dianetics, which embraces all fields of thought, and are being reeducated. It is found that they quickly desert the punishment-drive "therapies" as soon as they completely understand that they are not necessary, now that the natural laws of thought and behavior are known. One cannot, however, wholly repress a shudder at the fate of the hundreds of thousands of human guinea pigs whose lives and persons were ruined by the euthanistic methods employed in the dark ages of unreason.

Your health depends almost entirely upon your confidence in your ability to handle the physical universe about you and to change and adjust your environment so that you can survive in it. It is actually an illusion that you cannot ably handle your environment,

---

2.   subjugate: 1. to bring under control or subjection; conquer.

3.   dregs: 3. a small amount remaining; residue.

4.   tractable: 1. easily managed; docile; yielding.

5.   electric shock "therapy": there is no therapeutic reason for shocking anyone and there are no authentic cases on record of anyone having been cured of anything by shock.

an illusion implanted[6] by aberrated people in the past, during moments when you were unconscious and could not defend yourself or when you were small and were directed and misdirected and given pain and sorrow and upset, and had no way to effect your right to handle yourself in your environment.

On Lake Tanganyika[7] the natives have a very interesting way of catching fish. There on the equator the sun shines straight down through the clear water. The natives take blocks of wood and string them along a long rope. They stretch this rope between two canoes and with these abreast begin to paddle toward the shoal[8] water. By the time they have reached the shoals, schools of fish are piled and crowded into the rocks and onto the beach. The blocks of wood on the rope made shadows which went all the way down to the bottom of the lake and the fish, seeing the approach of these shadows and the apparent solid bars which they formed in the water, swam fearfully away from them and so were caught.

133

A man can be driven and harrassed and worked upon by aberrated people about him until he too conceives shadows to be reality. Should he simply reach out toward them, he would discover how thin and penetrable they are. His usual course, however, is to retreat from them and at last find himself in the shadows of bad health, broken dreams and an utter disownment of himself and the physical universe.

A considerable mechanical background of the action and peculiarities of the energy of thought makes it possible for these lists to bring about the improved state of being that they do, when properly used; but over and above these mechanical aspects, the simple recognition that there have been times in one's life when he did control the physical universe as needful, when he was in harmony with organisms about him, validates[9] the reality of his ability.

---

6.   implant: a painful and forceful means of overwhelming a being with artificial purpose or false concepts in a malicious attempt to control and suppress him.
7.   Tanganyika, Lake: 2. a lake in central Africa between Zaïre and Tanzania: the longest fresh-water lake in the world, about 450 miles long.
8.   shoal: 3. shallow.
9.   validate: 1. to make valid; substantiate; confirm.

134

Caught up by the illusion of words, stressed into obedience when he was a child by physical means, man is subject to his greatest shadow and illusion—*language*. The words, forcefully spoken, "Come here!" have no actual physical ability to draw the individual to the speaker. Yet he may approach, although he may be afraid to do so. He is impelled in his approach because he has been made to "come here" by physical force so many times in the early period of his life, while the words "come here" were being spoken, that he is trained much like a dog to obey a signal. The physical force which made him approach is lost to view and in its place stands the shadow "come here"; thus, to that degree he loses his self-determinism on the subject of "come here." As life goes on, he makes the great error of supposing that any and all words have force and importance. With words, those about him plant their shadow cages. They restrict him from doing this; they compel him to do that—and almost hour by hour and day by day he is directed by streams of words which in the ordinary society are not meant to help him but only to restrain him because of the fear of others. This Niagara[10] of language is effective only because it substitutes for periods when he was physically impelled against his wishes to accept things he did not want, to care for things for which he actually had no use or liking, to go where he did not wish to go, and to do what he did not want to do. Language is quite acceptable when understood as a *symbol* for the act and thing, but the word *ashtray* is no substitute for an ashtray. If you do not believe this, try to put your ashes on the air waves which have just carried the word *ashtray.* Called a *saucer* or an *elephant,* the object intended for ashes serves just as well.

By the trick of language, then, and a magical, wholly unsubstantial[11] trick it is, men seek to order the lives of men for their own advantage, and men caged about by the shadows observe and believe to their own detriment.[12]

All languages derive from observation of matter, energy, space and time and other organisms in the environment. There is no word which is not derived and which does not have the connotation[13] of the physical universe and other organisms.

---

10.   Niagara: a torrent, or flood.
11.   unsubstantial: 2. without material substance.
12.   detriment: 1. loss, damage, disadvantage, or injury.
13.   connotation: the implied meaning of an expression in addition to its primary meaning.

Thus, when you answer these questions by recalling incidents which they evoke,[14] be very sure that you do not evoke language incidents but action incidents. You do *not* want the time when you were *told* to do something—you want the time when you performed the *action.* You do not have to connect the language to the action in any way, but you will find as you answer questions on any of these lists that the value of language begins to depreciate[15] considerably and that language strangely enough will become much more useful to you.

135

Can you recall a time when:

☐ *Sight*
☐ *Smell*
☐ *Touch*
☐ *Color*
☐ *Tone*
☐ *External Motion*
☐ *Emotion*
☐ *Loudness*
☐ *Body Position*
☐ *Sound*
☐ *Weight*
☐ *Personal Motion*

1. You moved an object.

2. An object moved you.

3. You threw an organism up into the air.

4. You walked downstairs.

5. You acquired something you wanted.

6. You created something good.

7. You felt big in a certain space.

8. You were proud to move something heavy.

9. You handled energy well.

10. You built a fire.

11. You lost something you didn't want.

12. You forced something on somebody.

13. You promoted survival.

---

14. evoke: 1. to call up, produce or suggest (memories, feelings, etc.).
15. depreciate: 5. to decline in value.

14. You pleasantly expended time.

15. You closed in space.

16. You were master of your own time.

17. You opened up a space.

18. You handled a machine well.

136

☐ Sight
☐ Smell
☐ Touch
☐ Color
☐ Tone
☐ External
   Motion
☐ Emotion
☐ Loudness
☐ Body
   Position
☐ Sound
☐ Weight
☐ Personal
   Motion

19. You stopped a machine.

20. You raised an object.

21. You lowered yourself.

22. You destroyed something you didn't want.

23. You changed something for the better.

24. An organism you did not like moved away from you.

25. You obtained something you wanted.

26. You maintained a person.

27. You brought somebody you liked close to you.

28. You left a space you didn't like.

29. You conquered energy.

30. You destroyed a bad organism.

31. You handled fluid well.

32. You brought a number of pleasant objects together.

33. You placed a number of objects into space.

34. You threw unwanted objects away.

35. You dispersed many objects.

36. You tore an unwanted object to pieces.

37. You filled a space.

☐ Sight
☐ Smell
☐ Touch
☐ Color
☐ Tone
☐ External Motion
☐ Emotion
☐ Loudness
☐ Body Position
☐ Sound
☐ Weight
☐ Personal Motion

38. You regulated another's time.

39. You held an object close that you wanted.

40. You improved an object.

41. You emptied a space you wanted.

42. You went a distance.

43. You let time go.

44. You did what you wanted to do yourself.

45. You won out over an organism.

46. You got out from under domination.

47. You realized you were living your own life.

48. You knew you didn't have to do it.

49. You escaped from a dangerous space.

50. You entered upon a pleasant time.

138

Assists to Remembering

*R*emember is derived, of course, directly from ac-   139
tion in the physical universe. How would a deaf-mute teach a child
to remember? It would be necessary for him to keep forcing objects
or actions on the child when the child left them alone or omitted
them. Although parents are not deaf-mutes, children do not understand languages at very early ages, and as a consequence learn
to *remember* by having their attention first called toward actions and
objects, spaces and time. It violates the self-determinism of the
individual, and therefore his ability to handle himself, to have things
forced upon him without his agreement. This could be said to
account, in part, for some of the "poor memories" about which people
brag or complain.

Because one learns language at the level of the physical
universe and action within it, he could be said to do with his thoughts
what he has been compelled to do with the matter, energy, space and
time in his environment. Thus, if these have been forced upon him
and he did not want them, after a while he will begin to reject the
thoughts concerning these objects, but if these objects, spaces and
times and actions are forced upon him consistently enough he will at
length go into an apathy about them. He will not want them very
much but he thinks he has to accept them. Later on, in school,
his whole livelihood[1] seems to depend on whether or not he can
remember the "knowledge" which is forced upon him.

The physical universe level of remembering, then, is retaining matter, energy, space and time. To improve the memory, it
is only necessary to rehabilitate the individual's choice of acceptance
of the material universe.

---

1.   livelihood: means of living or of supporting life.

In answering these questions, particular attention should be paid to the happier incidents. Inevitably many unhappy incidents will flick through, but where selection is possible, happy or analytical incidents should be stressed. This list does not pertain to asking you to remember times when you remembered. It pertains to acquiring things which you wanted to acquire.

Can you remember a time when:

140

□ *Sight*
□ *Smell*
□ *Touch*
□ *Color*
□ *Tone*
□ *External Motion*
□ *Emotion*
□ *Loudness*
□ *Body Position*
□ *Sound*
□ *Weight*
□ *Personal Motion*

1. You acquired something you wanted.

2. You threw away something you didn't want.

3. You abandoned something you knew you were supposed to have.

4. You did something else with the time which was otherwise appointed[2] for you.

5. You went into a space you were not supposed to occupy.

6. You left the place you were supposed to be.

7. You were happy to have acquired something you couldn't afford.

8. You happily defied directions you had been given.

9. You were sent to one place and chose to go to another.

10. You chose your own clothing.

2.   appoint: 1. to fix or decide by authority.

11. You wore something in spite of what people would think.

12. You got rid of something which bored you.

13. You were glad to have choice over one of two objects.

14. You didn't drink any more than you wanted to.

☐ *Sight*
☐ *Smell*
☐ *Touch*
☐ *Color*
☐ *Tone*
☐ *External Motion*
☐ *Emotion*
☐ *Loudness*
☐ *Body Position*
☐ *Sound*
☐ *Weight*
☐ *Personal Motion*

15. You successfully refused to eat.

16. You did what you pleased with yourself.

17. You did what you pleased with a smaller person.

18. You were right not to have accepted something.

19. You gave away a present you had received.

20. You destroyed an object somebody forced upon you.

21. You had something you wanted and maintained it well.

22. You maliciously[3] scuffed your shoes.

23. You didn't read the book you had been given.

24. You refused to be owned.

25. You changed somebody's orders.

---

3. malicious: feeling or showing or caused by malice (a desire to harm others or to tease).

26. You slept where you pleased.

27. You refused to bathe.

28. You spoiled some clothing and were cheerful about it.

29. You got what you wanted.

30. You got back something you had lost.

142

31. You got the person you wanted.

32. You refused a partner.

33. You threw the blankets off the bed.

34. You had your own way.

35. You found you had been right in refusing it.

□ Sight
□ Smell
□ Touch
□ Color
□ Tone
□ External Motion
□ Emotion
□ Loudness
□ Body Position
□ Sound
□ Weight
□ Personal Motion

Forgetter Section

I t is generally conceded[1] that the opposite of *to* 143
remember is *to forget*. People can easily become confused between
these two things so that they forget what they think they should
remember and remember what they think they should forget. The
basic and underlying confusion between *forget* and *remember* has to
do, evidently, with what has been done to the individual on a
physical level and what has been forced on him or taken away from
him in terms of matter, energy, space and time.

The word *forget* rests for its definition on the action of
leaving something alone. How would a deaf-mute teach a child to
forget something? He would, of course, have to hide it or consistently
take it away from a child until the child went into apathy about it
and would have nothing further to do with it. If he did this enough,
so that the child would abandon the object, a child could be said to
have forgotten the object, since the child, or any person, will do with
his thoughts what he has done with the matter, energy, space, time
and organisms around him, thoughts being an approximation[2] in
symbological form of the physical universe. If a child has been
forcefully made to leave alone or abandon objects, energy, spaces and
times, later on when he hears the word *forget*, this means he must
abandon a certain thought and if he is in apathy concerning the
forced loss of objects or having them taken away from him in
childhood, he will proceed to forget them very thoroughly.

It could be said that an individual will occlude as many
thoughts as he has had to leave alone or lose objects in life. Pain itself
is a loss, being uniformly accompanied by the loss of cells of the body.
Thus the loss of objects or organisms by the individual can be

---

1. concede: 1. to acknowledge as true, just or proper; admit.
2. approximation: 3. a coming or getting near to identity in quantity, quality or degree; an approach
    to a correct estimate or conception of anything.

misconstrued[3] as being painful. Memories then can be called painful which actually contain no physical pain. But the individual must have had physical pain in order to understand that the loss means pain.

Punishment often accompanies, in child training, the times when the child is supposed to leave something alone. Thus, having to leave something alone is equivalent to being painful. Thus to remember something one is supposed to forget could be erroneously judged to be painful and indeed it is not.

There is a whole philosophy in existence that the best thing to do with unpleasant thoughts is to forget them. This is based securely upon an apathy occasioned by early training. A child when asking for an object will usually at first be cheerful and when he does not procure it will become angry; if he still does not procure it he may cry; and at last goes into apathy concerning it and says that he does not want it. This is one of the derivations[4] of the Dianetic tone scale and can be observed by anyone.

These questions, then, are an effort to overcome the times when one has had to leave things alone, when one has had to lose things, and when the loss has been enforced. Thus, when answering these questions, it would be very well to try to find several incidents for.each, particularly a very early incident.

Can you recall an incident when:

1. You put something aside because you thought it was dangerous but it wasn't.

2. You acquired something you were not supposed to have and kept it.

---

3.   misconstrue: to misinterpret.
4.   derivation: 3. the source from which something is derived; origin.

3. You cheerfully got into everything you were supposed to leave alone.

4. You went back to something you had been pulled away from.

5. You found the caution to leave something alone groundless.[5]

6. You cheerfully destroyed an expensive object.

7. You threw away something you wanted.

8. You played with somebody you were supposed to leave alone.

9. You were right in disobeying.

10. You read a forbidden book.

11. You enjoyed having things.

12. You acquired a dangerous object and enjoyed it.

13. You stole some food and were cheerful about it.

14. You ate exactly what you pleased.

15. You fixed some electrical wiring successfully.

16. You played with fire.

17. You successfully drove dangerously.

18. You touched something in spite of all warnings.

☐ *Sight*
☐ *Smell*
☐ *Touch*
☐ *Color*
☐ *Tone*
☐ *External Motion*
☐ *Emotion*
☐ *Loudness*
☐ *Body Position*
☐ *Sound*
☐ *Weight*
☐ *Personal Motion*

145

5.　groundless: without reason or cause; unjustified.

19. You got away with it.

20. She walked out on you.

21. You and some friends collected objects.

22. You touched a forbidden thing happily.

23. You got it anyway.

146

☐ *Sight*
☐ *Smell*
☐ *Touch*
☐ *Color*
☐ *Tone*
☐ *External Motion*
☐ *Emotion*
☐ *Loudness*
☐ *Body Position*
☐ *Sound*
☐ *Weight*
☐ *Personal Motion*

24. You went where you weren't supposed to and enjoyed it.

25. You owned something that was once forbidden.

26. He walked out on you.

27. You threw away something you had had to accept.

28. You found something which had been hidden from you.

29. You acquired a habit you weren't supposed to have and enjoyed it.

30. You were right and they were wrong.

31. You enjoyed yourself in a forbidden space.

32. You weren't supposed to do it and you did.

33. People were glad they had been wrong about you.

34. You recovered something somebody had thrown away.

35. You bullied somebody into giving you something you wanted.

36. You kept on with this processing despite what was said.

37. You persisted in doing something until they agreed you had a right to.

38. You suddenly realized you could do anything you wanted with an object.

147

- [ ] *Sight*
- [ ] *Smell*
- [ ] *Touch*
- [ ] *Color*
- [ ] *Tone*
- [ ] *External Motion*
- [ ] *Emotion*
- [ ] *Loudness*
- [ ] *Body Position*
- [ ] *Sound*
- [ ] *Weight*
- [ ] *Personal Motion*

39. You did something dangerous and got away with it.

40. Your group finally got something they had been denied.

41. You found you didn't have to sit there any more.

42. You realized you didn't have to go to school ever again.

43. You realized it was recess.[6]

44. You played hooky.

45. You made something look like something else.

46. You found where an adult had made a mistake.

47. You discovered it wasn't what they said it was.

48. You found yourself master of all of your possessions.

---

6.   recess: 3. a temporary withdrawal from or halting of work, business, study, etc.

148

☐ *Sight*

☐ *Smell*

☐ *Touch*

☐ *Color*

☐ *Tone*

☐ *External Motion*

☐ *Emotion*

☐ *Loudness*

☐ *Body Position*

☐ *Sound*

☐ *Weight*

☐ *Personal Motion*

49. You discovered you didn't necessarily have to go to sleep at night.

50. Although you felt you had to eat it, you left it alone.

51. You ate something that wasn't good for you and enjoyed it.

52. You let yourself get mad and were glad of it.

53. You suddenly decided you couldn't be that bad.

54. You opened a forbidden door.

55. You made it go very fast when it should have gone slow.

56. You stole some time.

57. You found some love you didn't know was there.

58. You abandoned somebody and were glad of it.

59. You refused to leave that time alone.

60. You sneaked off and built a fire.

61. You didn't realize it could be that good.

62. You found out it wasn't bad to play.

63. You couldn't see what was wrong with pleasure.

64. You left off doing something you were supposed to do to do something you enjoyed.

65. You acquired a space you once wouldn't have had.

66. You indulged yourself thoroughly.

67. They couldn't keep you back from it.

68. You successfully refused to come to the table.

69. You got burned anyway and didn't care.

70. You got rid of an object and acquired liberty.

149

☐ Sight
☐ Smell
☐ Touch
☐ Color
☐ Tone
☐ External Motion
☐ Emotion
☐ Loudness
☐ Body Position
☐ Sound
☐ Weight
☐ Personal Motion

150

Survival Factors

In that the basic drive of life is survival and in that   151
good survival must contain an abundance, the survival characteristics of people, organisms, matter, energy, space and time, from the viewpoint of an individual, are very important. The incentive toward survival is the acquisition of pleasure. The thrust away from death is the threat of pain. High ideals and ethics enhance the potentialities of the individual and the group in surviving. The ultimate in survival is immortality.

The factors which make up life can become contradictory in that one item can, in itself, assist survival and inhibit survival. A knife for instance is prosurvival in the hand, but contrasurvival when pointed at the breast by somebody else. As a person advances in life, he becomes confused as to the survival value of certain persons, various objects, energy, space and time. The individual desires survival for himself, for his family, for his children, for his group, for life in general and the physical universe. Confusing one thing with another and beholding[1] an item which was once survival become nonsurvival, beholding nonsurvival entities taking on survival qualities, the ability of the individual to evaluate his environment in terms of whether it assists or inhibits survival deteriorates.

An individual, a family, a group best survives, of course, when prosurvival entities are in proximity and available and when contrasurvival entities are absent. The struggle of life could be said to be the procurement of prosurvival factors and the annihilation,[2] destruction, banishment of contrasurvival factors.

---

1.   behold: to see, to observe.
2.   annihilate: 1. to destroy completely; put out of existence; demolish.

Emotion is directly regulated by prosurvival and contra-survival factors in life. When an individual procures and has in his proximity a strong survival entity such as another person or animal or object, he is *happy*. As this prosurvival entity departs from him, his emotional reaction deteriorates in direct ratio to his belief in his ability to recover it. As it threatens to depart he becomes *antagonistic* and fights to keep it near him. If its departure seems certain, he will become *angry* and lest[3] it become prosurvival for another life form and he is assured he has lost it, he will even destroy

152
it. When he realizes what his own state may be or the state of his family, children or group with his prosurvival entity departed he experiences *fear* that its loss will be permanent. When he recognizes what he believes to be a nearly irretrievable absence of this pro-survival entity he experiences *grief*. When it is considered to be lost permanently he experiences *apathy* and in apathy he may even go to the point of saying he did not want it. Actually, from an-tagonism on down the tone scale of emotion all the way to grief, he is still fighting to get it back and only in apathy abandons it and negates against it.

In the case of a person, animal, object, energy, space or time which threatens the survival of an individual, his family, his children or his group, the best survival can be accomplished when such an entity has been banished or destroyed or is as distant as possible from the individual, his family, his children or his group. In the case of the mad dog, the greatest danger exists when he is nearest and the greatest safety exists when he is most distant or absent. With contrasurvival objects, then, we have the tone scale in reverse. When the contrasurvival object is present and cannot be put away, the individual experiences apathy. When the individual believes himself to be threatened or when he feels his family, his children or his group are threatened by a contrasurvival object to a point where he cannot easily repel it, grief is experienced, for grief contains some hope of victory through enlisting[4] the sympathy of one's allies. When a contrasurvival entity is threatening to approach, fear is experienced, providing one feels that a direct attack is not possible. If the con-trasurvival object is near, but the individual, his family, his child-ren or his group feel that it can be conquered, even though it is

---

3.   lest: 1. in order that not, to avoid the risk of, lest we forget.
4.   enlist: 4. to secure (a person, services, etc.) for some cause, enterprise, etc.

already too close, anger results. If a contrasurvival entity might possibly approach, antagonism is demonstrated. Above this level contrasurvival objects may be more and more distant or easily handled up to the point where the individual can even be cheerful about them, at which time they are either absent or can be handled with ease.

Individuals get into a fixed emotional state about their environment when contrasurvival objects remain too statically[5] in their environment or when prosurvival objects are too difficult to obtain and cannot be procured or brought near or seem inclined to leave. Mixed with these emotional states is the confusion occasioned by a dulled ability to differentiate between the pro- and contrasurvival of an entity.

153

A parent is contrasurvival in that he punishes, is much too big and cannot be contributed to, which lessens the survival potentialities of a child. On the other hand, the same parent furnishing food, clothing and shelter, and also, but not least, being an entity which loves and can be loved, is a prosurvival entity. The parent entirely absent, then, is not a satisfactory survival state. The parent present is not a satisfactory survival state. Hence an indecision results and the individual demonstrates anxiety toward the parent. But this anxiety exists because of many hidden situations extending back to the beginning of an individual's life. The following questions are designed so as to permit the individual to reevaluate the prosurvival and contrasurvival nature of persons, animals, objects, energies, space and time in general.

Can you recall a time when:

1. A person you disliked was about.

2. An individual you liked stood above you.

3. You finally accepted a person you liked.

---

5.   static: 3. not changing.

4. You enjoyed accompanying a person you liked.

5. You were against a person you liked.

6. You acquired an individual you liked.

7. You and a person you liked engaged in a pleasant action.

154

☐ *Sight*
☐ *Smell*
☐ *Touch*
☐ *Color*
☐ *Tone*
☐ *External Motion*
☐ *Emotion*
☐ *Loudness*
☐ *Body Position*
☐ *Sound*
☐ *Weight*
☐ *Personal Motion*

8. Your action resulted in getting rid of somebody you didn't like.

9. You enjoyed seeing somebody you admired.

10. You advanced toward a person you liked.

11. You acquired an object which you adored.

12. You knew somebody felt affection for you.

13. You got away from a person of whom you were afraid.

14. You walked after a person you liked.

15. A person you liked aided you.

16. You and people you liked were all together.

17. You almost met somebody you disliked.

18. You were glad to be alone.

19. Somebody aided your ambition.

20. You were among people you liked.

21. You found somebody amiable.

22. A person amused you.

23. You finally didn't have to be anxious.

24. A person you liked appeared suddenly.

☐ *Sight*
☐ *Smell*
☐ *Touch*
☐ *Color*
☐ *Tone*
☐ *External Motion*
☐ *Emotion*
☐ *Loudness*
☐ *Body Position*
☐ *Sound*
☐ *Weight*
☐ *Personal Motion*

25. You had a good appetite.

155

26. You approached somebody you honored.

27. Somebody approved of you.

28. A person you liked arose.

29. You were arrested[6] by somebody's beauty.

30. You enjoyed an arrival.

31. You found out you didn't have to be ashamed.

32. Somebody you liked was asleep.

33. You assailed[7] an enemy successfully.

34. A person you honored assisted you.

35. You enjoyed an associate.

36. You felt assured by a person you liked.

37. You were astonished to find out somebody respected you after all.

---

6.   arrest: 2. to attract and hold. 3. to check the course of; stop or slow down.
7.   assail: 1. to set upon with violence; assault.

38. You attacked somebody you didn't like.

39. You were attached to a friend.

40. Somebody you liked gave you attention.

41. You were attractive to somebody.

156

□ *Sight*
□ *Smell*
□ *Touch*
□ *Color*
□ *Tone*
□ *External Motion*
□ *Emotion*
□ *Loudness*
□ *Body Position*
□ *Sound*
□ *Weight*
□ *Personal Motion*

42. You were awakened by somebody of whom you were fond.

43. You were glad to find somebody was bad.

44. You played ball.

45. You played a battle with children.

46. Somebody considered you beautiful.

47. You discovered you had become fond of someone.

48. Somebody you disliked begged you.

49. You began a friendship.

50. You discovered you didn't have to behave.

51. A person you disliked was behind you.

52. You were below somebody you liked.

53. Somebody of whom you were fond bested you.

54. You were beside your favorite friend.

55. You discovered you were liked better than you thought.

56. You were between two friends.

57. You bit somebody you disliked.

58. You decided to be blind to a fault.

59. You liked somebody who was black.

☐ Sight
☐ Smell
☐ Touch
☐ Color
☐ Tone
☐ External Motion
☐ Emotion
☐ Loudness
☐ Body Position
☐ Sound
☐ Weight
☐ Personal Motion

157

60. Somebody asked you to blow hard.

61. Somebody's question made you blush pleasantly.

62. Somebody made you feel bold.

63. You were glad somebody had been born.

64. Nobody could bother you.

65. You had reached the bottom and started up.

66. You bowed to a friend.

67. You were in a box with a pleasant person.

68. You broke bread with somebody you liked.

69. You breakfasted with somebody you liked.

70. You liked somebody so much you could hardly breathe.

71. You brought somebody a present.

72. You brushed against somebody you liked.

73. Somebody helped you build something.

74. Somebody kissed a burn.

75. You were so happy you felt you would burst.

158

☐ Sight
☐ Smell
☐ Touch
☐ Color
☐ Tone
☐ External Motion
☐ Emotion
☐ Loudness
☐ Body Position
☐ Sound
☐ Weight
☐ Personal Motion

76. You buried something you didn't want.

77. You were too busy to see an enemy.

78. You stood by somebody.

79. You saw something you disliked in a cage.

80. You answered a call from a friend.

81. You broke a cane.

82. You captured an enemy.

83. You no longer had to be careful.

84. You found somebody cared.

85. You enjoyed being careless.

86. A cat you didn't like walked away from you.

87. You discovered you weren't the cause.

88. They couldn't catch you and you realized it.

89. You were certain of a friend.

90. You discovered you had charm.

91. You enjoyed a child.

92. You found a church pleasant.

93. You discovered there were friends in the city.

94. You and others left the classroom.

☐ Sight
☐ Smell
☐ Touch
☐ Color
☐ Tone
☐ External Motion
☐ Emotion
☐ Loudness
☐ Body Position
☐ Sound
☐ Weight
☐ Personal Motion

95. Somebody believed you clever.

96. You found an enemy was clumsy.

97. You didn't have to clothe yourself as directed.

98. You threw away a collar.

99. You didn't have to comb your hair.

100. You were comfortable with a person.

101. You saw an enemy coming and didn't meet him.

102. You could come as you pleased.

103. An enemy had to obey your command.

104. You found you were in command.

105. You heard an enemy was committed.[8]

106. You were in good company.

107. You took compassion on an enemy.

---

8.   commit: 3c. to expose to risk or danger.

108. You were discovered to be a good companion.

109. You felt complete.

110. You concealed yourself from an enemy.

111. You condemned an enemy.

112. People had confidence in you.

160

☐ Sight
☐ Smell
☐ Touch
☐ Color
☐ Tone
☐ External Motion
☐ Emotion
☐ Loudness
☐ Body Position
☐ Sound
☐ Weight
☐ Personal Motion

113. You confounded⁹ an enemy.

114. You conquered an enemy physically.

115. Somebody consented.

116. You couldn't contain¹⁰ yourself.

117. You saw an enemy contract.

118. You proved¹¹ very contrary.

119. It was hard to count your friends.

120. People realized you had courage.

121. Your courting¹² was successful.

122. You put a cover¹³ over an enemy.

123. You made an enemy crawl.

124. You created a group.

125. You made somebody get over being cross.

9.   confound: 1. to perplex or amaze; confuse.
10.   contain: 4. to keep under proper control; restrain.
11.   prove: 10. to be found by trial or experience to be.
12.   court: 15. to seek the affections of.
13.   cover: a commanding position with regard to.

126. You were glad to be in a crowd.

127. You made an enemy cry.

128. You cured a friend.

129. An enemy cut himself.

130. You lost an enemy in the dark.

☐ Sight
☐ Smell
☐ Touch
☐ Color
☐ Tone
☐ External
   Motion
☐ Emotion
☐ Loudness
☐ Body
   Position
☐ Sound
☐ Weight
☐ Personal
   Motion

131. You discovered something you didn't like was dead.

132. You turned a deaf ear to an enemy.

133. You forgave somebody for deceiving you.

134. You threw somebody you didn't like into dejection.

135. You delayed a catastrophe.

136. Somebody was delighted with you.

137. You could not deny a favor.

138. You could not deny what you wanted.

139. You overlooked a defect in a friend.

140. You were depended upon.

141. An enemy got what he deserved.

142. Your desire was answered.

143. You departed from an enemy.

144. An enemy departed from you.

145. You drove an enemy into despair.

146. You and another successfully reached a destination.

147. Your group destroyed an enemy.

148. Your determination won.

149. You could tell the difference.

150. You diminished an enemy.

162

□ Sight
□ Smell
□ Touch
□ Color
□ Tone
□ External
    Motion
□ Emotion
□ Loudness
□ Body
    Position
□ Sound
□ Weight
□ Personal
    Motion

151. You dispersed a group you didn't like.

152. You found you were right to distrust somebody.

153. You dived in.

154. There was plenty to divide.

155. You had no doubt of someone.

156. You drove somebody.

157. You and a friendly person ate.

158. Your effort was rewarded.

159. You were enclosed by friends.

160. You successfully encouraged somebody.

161. You put an end to something you didn't like.

162. You enjoyed watching somebody leave.

163. You knew you'd had enough and took action.

164. Somebody was entranced with you.

165. You were equal to anyone.

166. You escaped from an enemy.

167. You got even with somebody you didn't like.

168. You passed an examination in spite of somebody.

169. You were excited by an arrival.

163

170. Somebody you didn't like escaped from you.

171. Somebody you disliked went far away.

172. You discovered a person had been faithful.

173. You discovered you didn't have to be afraid any more.

174. You fed somebody.

175. You discovered your enemies were few.

176. You found somebody you had been looking for.

177. You decided to stick to the finish.

178. Your first enemy went away from you.

179. You watched a detested person flee.

180. You forbade somebody to come near you and were obeyed.

☐ Sight
☐ Smell
☐ Touch
☐ Color
☐ Tone
☐ External Motion
☐ Emotion
☐ Loudness
☐ Body Position
☐ Sound
☐ Weight
☐ Personal Motion

181. You used force on somebody successfully.

182. You realized you were free.

183. You knew you had a friend.

184. You frightened somebody you didn't like.

185. You gathered friends together.

164

☐ *Sight*
☐ *Smell*
☐ *Touch*
☐ *Color*
☐ *Tone*
☐ *External Motion*
☐ *Emotion*
☐ *Loudness*
☐ *Body Position*
☐ *Sound*
☐ *Weight*
☐ *Personal Motion*

186. You could go outside the gate.

187. People found you generous.

188. You no longer had to be on your guard.

189. People made you happy.

190. You harmed a person you didn't like.

191. Somebody you liked hastened to you.

192. You healed a friend.

193. You helped an ally.

194. You had a friend.

195. You hindered an enemy.

196. Somebody tossed you up high.

197. You put an enemy in the hole.

198. You agreed it was hot.

199. You hunted an enemy.

200. You hurried toward a group.

201. You hurt somebody you needed.

202. You coaxed somebody into being idle.

203. You illuminated[14] a group.

204. You discovered you had imagined a wrong about someone.

205. You and a friend did the impossible.

☐ Sight
☐ Smell
☐ Touch
☐ Color
☐ Tone
☐ External Motion
☐ Emotion
☐ Loudness
☐ Body Position
☐ Sound
☐ Weight
☐ Personal Motion

165

206. Somebody you had hunted walked in.

207. You found an enemy ignorant.

208. You made somebody you didn't like impatient.

209. You were discovered to be interesting.

210. Your invention was appreciated.

211. You took a pleasant journey.

212. You made somebody joyful.

213. You jumped.

214. You kept somebody from doing wrong.

215. You saw an enemy kicked out.

216. You overcame a desire to kill.

217. Somebody found you were kind.

218. You were first kissed.

219. You landed on your feet.

220. You were late and it didn't matter.

---

14.   illuminate: 4. to enlighten, as with knowledge.

221. You made people laugh.

222. You and a person you liked were lazy.

223. You left an enemy.

224. There was one less.

225. You caught an enemy in a lie.

166

□ *Sight*
□ *Smell*
□ *Touch*
□ *Color*
□ *Tone*
□ *External Motion*
□ *Emotion*
□ *Loudness*
□ *Body Position*
□ *Sound*
□ *Weight*
□ *Personal Motion*

226. You and your group enjoyed life.

227. You were glad it was light.

228. You were happy to listen.

229. You overcame somebody bigger than you.

230. You made somebody glad to be alive.

231. You found love really existed.

232. Your luck was excellent.

233. You fixed a machine for somebody.

234. You received pleasant mail.

235. You knew a good man.

236. Somebody imitated your manner.

237. You had an enemy under your control.

238. You decided not to marry.

239. You found you were the master.

240. You discovered you weren't mean.

241. You had a happy meeting.

242. You were in the midst of friends.

243. A person you didn't like minded you.

244. A friend interested you with music.

245. People found you mysterious.

246. You discovered nobody disliked you.

247. You could make all the noise you pleased.

□ Sight
□ Smell
□ Touch
□ Color
□ Tone
□ External Motion
□ Emotion
□ Loudness
□ Body Position
□ Sound
□ Weight
□ Personal Motion

167

248. You didn't have to obey.

249. You obliged somebody.

250. You discovered you had not been observed after all.

251. You made it a gala[15] occasion.

252. You offended somebody you didn't like.

253. You sat on somebody.

254. You shut the door on an enemy.

255. You disobeyed an order and found it was all right.

256. You organized a game.

257. You were glad to participate.

258. You were happy in[16] a partner.

259. You took somebody's part.

15. gala: 1. festive; showy.
16. in: 10. with respect to.

260. Somebody experienced passion for you.

261. You were patient with a foolish person.

262. You brought peace.

263. You felt pity for an enemy.

168

□ Sight
□ Smell
□ Touch
□ Color
□ Tone
□ External
    Motion
□ Emotion
□ Loudness
□ Body
    Position
□ Sound
□ Weight
□ Personal
    Motion

264. You were impolite and it served your purpose.

265. You found you weren't poor.

266. You took position beside a friend.

267. You felt powerful in your friends.

268. You found somebody was precious to you.

269. You did what you preferred to do with a person.

270. You gave somebody you liked a present.

271. You prevented somebody from doing something foolish.

272. Somebody thought you were pretty.

273. You found you didn't want to see somebody go to prison.

274. You were right in standing by your principles.

275. You were part of a procession.

276. They discovered you could produce.

277. You and a friend made progress.

278. Somebody was true to a promise.

279. Proof wasn't necessary.

280. Somebody was proud of you.

281. You stayed with your purpose.   169

☐ Sight
☐ Smell
☐ Touch
☐ Color
☐ Tone
☐ External Motion
☐ Emotion
☐ Loudness
☐ Body Position
☐ Sound
☐ Weight
☐ Personal Motion

282. You were discovered to be of good quality.

283. You stopped a quarrel.

284. You found you could act quickly.

285. It was unnecessary to be quiet.

286. You lifted a child.

287. You discovered enmity[17] was rare.

288. Somebody read to you.

289. There was danger and you were ready.

290. Somebody unexpectedly reappeared.

291. You received somebody you liked.

292. You recognized a friend.

293. Somebody took refuge in you.

294. You discovered your regrets were in vain.

295. People rejoiced with you.

---

17. enmity: a feeling or condition of hostility; hatred; ill will; animosity; antagonism.

296. A friend rejoined you.

297. A person decided to remain.

298. You were considered remarkable.

299. You repeated something and weren't sorry for it.

300. People found you had been wrongly represented.

170

☐ Sight
☐ Smell
☐ Touch
☐ Color
☐ Tone
☐ External Motion
☐ Emotion
☐ Loudness
☐ Body Position
☐ Sound
☐ Weight
☐ Personal Motion

301. Somebody said you resembled somebody.

302. You found you didn't have to respect somebody.

303. You restored a friendship.

304. You retained good will.

305. You revealed trickery.

306. A friend rubbed against you.

307. You tried to save somebody you disliked from ruin.

308. You made an unfriendly person run.

309. You cured somebody's sadness.

310. You discovered safety.

311. You knew you were part of a pretty scene.

312. You were right in claiming somebody was a scoundrel.

313. You made an unfriendly person scream.

314. You were happy to find somebody wasn't what he seemed.

315. You found you didn't think about yourself all the time after all.

316. You sent somebody away.

317. You found a person wasn't as severe as you had thought.

318. You made somebody shake.

319. You shouted with joy.

320. You enjoyed shutting something up.

321. You had a friend at your side.

322. You enjoyed the sight of a person leaving.

323. You forced silence.

324. You found your size didn't matter.

325. Somebody found you were skillful.

326. You were glad you had been slow.

327. You succeeded in putting a puzzle together.

328. You were glad something was slippery.

329. You were glad you came too soon.

☐ Sight
☐ Smell
☐ Touch
☐ Color
☐ Tone
☐ External Motion
☐ Emotion
☐ Loudness
☐ Body Position
☐ Sound
☐ Weight
☐ Personal Motion

330. Somebody was sore at you and it didn't do any good.

331. You tied somebody to a stake.

332. You enjoyed startling somebody.

333. You found you didn't have to starve.

334. You didn't want to stay and didn't.

172

☐ Sight
☐ Smell
☐ Touch
☐ Color
☐ Tone
☐ External Motion
☐ Emotion
☐ Loudness
☐ Body Position
☐ Sound
☐ Weight
☐ Personal Motion

335. Somebody stuck to you.

336. Somebody was still your friend.

337. Somebody stirred[18] you.

338. You stopped over to talk to somebody.

339. You stopped an unfriendly person.

340. Somebody you liked in a store was good to you.

341. Somebody made you feel less strong.

342. You stripped[19] an unfriendly person.

343. Somebody stroked you.

344. Somebody discovered how strong you were.

345. You won a struggle.

346. You subdued an unkind person.

347. You found you had a subject.

348. You made an unfriendly person submit.

---

18.   stir: 3. to arouse or excite or stimulate.
19.   strip: 2. to deprive or dispossess (a person or thing) of (honors, titles, attributes, etc.).

349. You succeeded in spite of people.

350. You made a person suffer with justice.

351. You gave another person a suit.

352. You felt sure in the presence of somebody.

353. You handled somebody well.

354. You seized an unfriendly person.

355. Your search was rewarded.

356. Somebody tried to send you away and you didn't go.

357. You found you had taken somebody too seriously.

358. You watched an unfriendly person move fast.

359. You found shame wasn't necessary.

360. Somebody discovered they had suspected you wrongly.

361. You should have told and you did.

362. Your anxiety was for nothing.

363. You apprehended an unfriendly person.

364. You were glad somebody was tall.

365. Your tears were followed by relief.

366. You terrified an unfriendly person.

☐ Sight
☐ Smell
☐ Touch
☐ Color
☐ Tone
☐ External Motion
☐ Emotion
☐ Loudness
☐ Body Position
☐ Sound
☐ Weight
☐ Personal Motion

173

367. They had to admit you hadn't stolen it after all.

368. Somebody had to respect your rights of ownership.

369. You tried an unfriendly person out.

370. You got together with an unfriendly person and won.

174

☐ Sight
☐ Smell
☐ Touch
☐ Color
☐ Tone
☐ External Motion
☐ Emotion
☐ Loudness
☐ Body Position
☐ Sound
☐ Weight
☐ Personal Motion

371. You treated many people.

372. You were glad it was true.

373. You found it was all right to be under someone.

374. You discovered you weren't an unhappy person.

375. You discovered the difference between *no* and *know*.

376. You lifted up a child.

377. You enjoyed going upstairs with somebody.

378. You were found to be useful.

379. Something you thought was rare turned out to be usual.

380. You discovered it was all right to be vain.

381. They discovered how valuable you were.

382. You found something wasn't a vice.[20]

383. You recovered your vigor.

384. You overcame a violent person.

385. You found you had no invisible enemies.

386. You made a dog wag his tail.

□ Sight
□ Smell
□ Touch
□ Color
□ Tone
□ External Motion
□ Emotion
□ Loudness
□ Body Position
□ Sound
□ Weight
□ Personal Motion

387. You really earned the wages you were paid.

388. You made an enemy wait.

389. You walked with somebody you liked.

390. You backed an unfriendly person up against a wall.

391. You wandered happily.

392. Somebody found you were warm.

393. You found it was all right to watch.

394. You discovered you were not weak.

395. You made an unfriendly person weep.

396. You did not care where he went.

397. You were happy to watch somebody go.

398. You physically compelled somebody to come.

399. You had a good opinion of a wife.

---

20.   vice: 1. evil or grossly immoral conduct, great wickedness.

400. You had a good opinion of a husband.

401. You discovered it wasn't wrong.

402. You did something wrong and it turned out all right.

403. You were complimented on writing.

404. You made somebody yell.

176

☐ *Sight*
☐ *Smell*
☐ *Touch*
☐ *Color*
☐ *Tone*
☐ *External Motion*
☐ *Emotion*
☐ *Loudness*
☐ *Body Position*
☐ *Sound*
☐ *Weight*
☐ *Personal Motion*

405. Pleasant objects were against you.

406. You were glad an object was about.

407. Objects were all about you and you were happy.

408. You were glad an object was above you.

409. Somebody accepted an object you wanted to give.

410. One object accompanied another.

411. You acquired an object you wanted.

412. You got action out of objects.

413. Somebody admired something you had.

414. An object advanced[21] you.

415. You found an object adorned[22] you.

416. You discovered affection for something you had not known you liked.

---

21. advance: 2. to raise in rank or position: promote.
22. adorn: 1a. to make pleasing or attractive.

417. You threw something away of which you were afraid.

418. You ran after an object and caught it.

419. Something aided you.

420. You were glad to get rid of all of something.

□ *Sight*
□ *Smell*
□ *Touch*
□ *Color*
□ *Tone*
□ *External Motion*
□ *Emotion*
□ *Loudness*
□ *Body Position*
□ *Sound*
□ *Weight*
□ *Personal Motion*

177

421. An object almost injured you but you were all right.

422. You attained an ambition for something.

423. You were among pleasant objects.

424. You found an animal was amiable.

425. You amused somebody with an object.

426. You were anxious about something and got rid of it.

427. A dangerous object approached and you got it away.

428. Somebody approved of something.

429. You arrested an object.

430. You were glad to be a rival of an object.

431. You were happy a car came.

432. You found you hadn't been ashamed without cause.

433. You put an animal to sleep.

434. You assailed something victoriously.

435. You assisted somebody with something.

436. You stopped associating with something you didn't like.

437. An object gave you assurance.

438. You astonished people with something.

439. You attacked something successfully.

440. You attracted an object.

441. You threw a ball up.

442. You considered something beautiful.

443. Somebody begged you for something.

444. You made a machine behave.

445. You were glad you were behind something.

446. You were happy to be below something.

447. You didn't believe in an object.

448. You were between two objects.

449. You blew something out.

450. You scraped bottom.

451. You acquired bread.

452. You polished an object.

178

- [ ] Sight
- [ ] Smell
- [ ] Touch
- [ ] Color
- [ ] Tone
- [ ] External Motion
- [ ] Emotion
- [ ] Loudness
- [ ] Body Position
- [ ] Sound
- [ ] Weight
- [ ] Personal Motion

453. You burned something you didn't want.

454. You buried something you disliked.

455. You captured something.

456. You did something skillful with a car.

457. You found out you didn't have to be careful with an object.

458. You were successfully careless.

459. You charmed somebody with something.

460. You became certain about something.

461. You took care of some possession because you wanted to.

462. You saw something coming in time.

463. You exerted your command over an object.

464. You concealed something.

465. You condemned an object.

466. You gave somebody something and it gave them confidence.

467. You resolved an object which had confounded you.

468. You conquered an object.

469. Something was given away with your consent.

□ Sight
□ Smell
□ Touch
□ Color
□ Tone
□ External Motion
□ Emotion
□ Loudness
□ Body Position
□ Sound
□ Weight
□ Personal Motion

179

470. You constructed something well.

471. You arranged something that was very convenient.

472. You showed courage about an object.

473. You cut something you didn't want.

474. You got rid of an unwanted object.

180

475. You delayed a physical action.

476. An item gave you delight.

477. You denied something existed.

478. You depended on an object.

479. You were happy to receive something you deserved.

480. You watched an unwanted object depart.

481. You took delight in destroying something.

482. You saw the difference between two objects.

483. You watched an object diminish.

484. You did something which others considered too difficult.

485. You were happy to dig.

486. You dispersed many objects.

487. You mastered something you distrusted.

488. You did what you pleased with something.

489. You understood an object you had doubted.

490. You drew something to you.

491. You gave an animal a drink.

492. You watched an object drop.

☐ Sight
☐ Smell
☐ Touch
☐ Color
☐ Tone
☐ External
   Motion
☐ Emotion
☐ Loudness
☐ Body
   Position
☐ Sound
☐ Weight
☐ Personal
   Motion

493. You dwelled in a pleasant place.

494. You waited eagerly.

495. Something looked too good to eat.

496. You succeeded in moving an object after a great deal of effort.

497. You enclosed an object.

498. Something encouraged you.

499. You made an end to an object.

500. You found an object considered an enemy was really a friend.

501. You enjoyed possessing something.

502. You felt you couldn't get enough of something.

503. You cut an entrance.

504. You escaped from an object.

505. You successfully examined something dangerous.

506. You were excited by something.

507. You exercised an animal.

508. You turned an object on its face.

509. An object was faithful.

510. You threw something far from you.

182

☐ Sight
☐ Smell
☐ Touch
☐ Color
☐ Tone
☐ External
     Motion
☐ Emotion
☐ Loudness
☐ Body
     Position
☐ Sound
☐ Weight
☐ Personal
     Motion

511. You made something go fast.

512. You overcame the fear of an object.

513. You fed an animal.

514. You took the first thing that came to you without qualms.[23]

515. You made an object fit.

516. You watched somebody flee from an object and then approached it.

517. You owned something you had been forbidden to touch.

518. You successfully applied force.

519. You were proud of your possessions.

520. An object was a friend.

521. You frightened somebody with an object.

522. You happily gathered objects together.

523. You made something grow.

524. You were generous with objects.

---

23.   qualm: 2. a sudden feeling of uneasiness or doubt; misgiving.

525. You guarded something well.

526. An item made you very happy.

527. You were glad to do something harmful with an object.

528. You healed an animal.

529. You helped somebody with an object.

530. You found something somebody had hidden from you.

531. You hindered something bad.

532. You put a hole through an object.

533. You made an object very hot.

534. You hunted successfully.

535. You hurried to get something you wanted and achieved it.

536. You made an object hurt an enemy.

537. An object let you be idle.

538. You made something illuminate something.

539. You imagined a new object and made it.

540. You did the impossible with an object.

541. You watched something come in.

542. You increased your possessions.

□ Sight
□ Smell
□ Touch
□ Color
□ Tone
□ External Motion
□ Emotion
□ Loudness
□ Body Position
□ Sound
□ Weight
□ Personal Motion

543. Out of your own choice you took one object instead of another.

544. An object held your interest.

545. Somebody was happy with your invention.

546. You killed something bad.

184

☐ Sight
☐ Smell
☐ Touch
☐ Color
☐ Tone
☐ External Motion
☐ Emotion
☐ Loudness
☐ Body Position
☐ Sound
☐ Weight
☐ Personal Motion

547. You made an object jump.

548. You found that something was really yours.

549. You kissed an object out of happiness.

550. It was good that an object came too late.

551. You made somebody laugh with an object.

552. You took the length and breadth of an object.

553. You found an object lying.

554. You gave something life.

555. You lighted up a space well.

556. You were glad something was little.

557. You loved an object and kept it.

558. You managed a machine another couldn't manage.

559. You controlled an object.

560. You made an object make music.

561. You wrested[24] a secret from some mysterious object.

562. You were glad to be mean to an object.

563. You mastered an intricate item.

564. You watched the meeting of two objects.

☐ Sight
☐ Smell
☐ Touch
☐ Color
☐ Tone
☐ External Motion
☐ Emotion
☐ Loudness
☐ Body Position
☐ Sound
☐ Weight
☐ Personal Motion

565. You threw fluid up into the air.

566. You heated a fluid.

567. You poured a fluid out.

568. You mixed two fluids.

569. You stirred a fluid.

570. You found something wasn't necessary.

571. You made an animal obey you.

572. You obliged somebody with an object.

573. You bought something for an occasion.

574. You shut up an object.

575. You organized a number of items well.

576. You discovered the origin of something.

577. You inflicted pain with an object and were glad to do so.

578. You put an object in your pocket.

---

24.   wrest: 3. to get by effort.

579. An object made you feel rich.

580. You gave somebody something which was precious.

581. You prepared a mixture which was successful.

582. You preferred one object to the other.

186

☐ Sight
☐ Smell
☐ Touch
☐ Color
☐ Tone
☐ External Motion
☐ Emotion
☐ Loudness
☐ Body Position
☐ Sound
☐ Weight
☐ Personal Motion

583. You prevented harm from coming to an object.

584. You won a quarrel about an object.

585. You collected rain.

586. You acquired a fluid you wanted.

587. You raised an object.

588. You maintained something rare.

589. You were glad to receive something.

590. You recognized an object that puzzled others.

591. You gave an animal refuge.

592. You controlled an animal.

593. You restored an object.

594. You let somebody retain something valuable.

595. You made something run where others had failed.

596. You took an object to safety.

597. You put an object into something.

598. You took an object out of something.

599. You acquired something that was scarce.

600. You repaired a scratch on an object.

601. You made somebody scream with an object.

602. Someone found they had been too severe about an object.

603. You shook fluid off something.

604. You pulled an animal out of water.

605. You acquired an animal for food.

606. You tied an animal to a stake.

607. You struggled successfully with an object.

608. You stroked an object.

609. You were too strong for an object.

610. Something was submitted to you as a tribute.[25]

611. People discovered you were to be congratulated about an object.

612. You handled an object well.

613. You seized an object.

614. Your search for an object was rewarded.

□ Sight
□ Smell
□ Touch
□ Color
□ Tone
□ External Motion
□ Emotion
□ Loudness
□ Body Position
□ Sound
□ Weight
□ Personal Motion

187

---

25.   tribute: 1. something said or done or given as a mark of respect or admiration, etc.

615. You were glad to see an object.

616. You maintained something.

617. You overcame something which had threatened you.

618. You stopped an object from being noisy.

188

☐ *Sight*
☐ *Smell*
☐ *Touch*
☐ *Color*
☐ *Tone*
☐ *External Motion*
☐ *Emotion*
☐ *Loudness*
☐ *Body Position*
☐ *Sound*
☐ *Weight*
☐ *Personal Motion*

619. You convinced someone of the value of an object.

620. You squandered[26] some money.

621. You acquired some money.

622. You refused some money you didn't have coming.

623. You watched an unwanted object go.

624. You watched a desired object come.

625. You made something fly.

626. You left a space you didn't like.

627. You acquired a space you wanted.

628. You admired an area.

629. You advanced through space.

630. You felt affection for a space.

631. You were against a space.

632. You decorated a space.

---

26.   squander: to spend wastefully.

633. You were glad to get out of a space of which you were afraid.

634. You aided in making space.

635. You were pleasantly alone in space.

636. You were in an amusing space.

637. You conquered a distance.

☐ Sight
☐ Smell
638. You got through an unwholesome space.
☐ Touch
☐ Color
☐ Tone
639. You arrived in a pleasant space.
☐ External
   Motion
640. You opened up a space.
☐ Emotion
☐ Loudness
641. You gave another assurance about a space.
☐ Body
   Position
☐ Sound
642. You were attracted to a space.
☐ Weight
☐ Personal
   Motion
643. You awakened in a pleasant place.

644. You burned off a space.

645. You blindly, but successfully, got through an area.

646. You enjoyed a black space.

647. You made a box.

648. You went into a pleasant place.

649. You took something out of a place.

650. You filled a place full.

651. You enjoyed a box.

189

652. You let a space be occupied.

653. You broke into a forbidden space.

654. You made a good cage.

655. You captured an area.

656. You took a child out of a place.

190   □ *Sight*   657. You straightened up a space.
        □ *Smell*
        □ *Touch*   658. You liked jumping through space.
        □ *Color*
        □ *Tone*   659. You went below in space.
        □ *External*
          Motion   660. You made a broad space.
        □ *Emotion*
        □ *Loudness*   661. You collected many things in a place.
        □ *Body*
          Position   662. You created heat.
        □ *Sound*
        □ *Weight*   663. You brought a light.
        □ *Personal*
          Motion   664. You extinguished unfriendly energy.

665. You lit a light.

666. You regulated fire.

667. You successfully applied energy.

668. You burned something you didn't want.

669. You arranged lighting well.

670. You boiled something.

671. You made a machine run.

672. You dissipated heat.

673. You chilled something.

674. You went from a dark place into a friendly lighted one.

675. You were glad it was dark.

676. You left darkness behind you.

677. You were happy with the sunrise.

☐ *Sight*

☐ *Smell*   678. You watched twilight fade.

☐ *Touch*

☐ *Color*   679. You saw lighted windows.

☐ *Tone*

☐ *External*   680. You found something with a light.
   Motion

☐ *Emotion*   681. You were glad to enter a warm place.

☐ *Loudness*

☐ *Body*   682. You made a cold place warm.
   Position

☐ *Sound*   683. You warmed somebody.

☐ *Weight*

☐ *Personal*   684. You heated something to eat.
   Motion

685. You found companionship in fire.

686. You found somebody was warm against you.

687. You were glad to leave a cold place.

688. You made a barren place pleasant.

689. You found someone waiting for you in a dark place and were glad.

690. You regulated time well.

691. You left a bad time behind you.

692. You approached a good time.

693. You decided that things had not been so bad.

694. You found your time well spent.

695. You utilized some time yesterday.

696. You enjoyed a time today.

192

☐ *Sight*
☐ *Smell*
☐ *Touch*
☐ *Color*
☐ *Tone*
☐ *External Motion*
☐ *Emotion*
☐ *Loudness*
☐ *Body Position*
☐ *Sound*
☐ *Weight*
☐ *Personal Motion*

Imagination

One of the most important parts of the thinking   193
process is imagination. Imagination is actually a form of computation. Imagination gives calculated and instinctive solutions for
the future. If an imagination is dulled, one's computation is seriously
handicapped. Imagination is a good thing, not a bad thing. With
daydreaming, for instance, a person can convert a not-too-pleasant
existence into something livable. Only with imagination can one
postulate future goals to attain.

Can you recall a time when:

□ *Sight*
□ *Smell*
□ *Touch*
□ *Color*
□ *Tone*
□ *External Motion*
□ *Emotion*
□ *Loudness*
□ *Body Position*
□ *Sound*
□ *Weight*
□ *Personal Motion*

1. You foresaw how something should be and so arranged it.

2. You imagined something and constructed it.

3. You envisioned how a place would look and went there.

4. You were forced to admit you lied when you had told the truth.

5. Somebody disarranged what was yours and you put it back.

6. You delighted in filling up space with imaginary things.

7. You did a masterpiece of creation.

8. You saw something come into actuality which you had imagined.

9. You imagined it was there and destroyed it.

10. Your vision was complimented.

194

☐ *Sight*
☐ *Smell*
☐ *Touch*
☐ *Color*
☐ *Tone*
☐ *External Motion*
☐ *Emotion*
☐ *Loudness*
☐ *Body Position*
☐ *Sound*
☐ *Weight*
☐ *Personal Motion*

11. You planned what to do with some time and did it.

12. You ignored interruptions and went on according to schedule.

13. You saw how some space could be bettered and bettered it.

14. You drew a plan and people followed it.

15. Things were smoother because you had thought of them that way.

16. You made profit out of imagination.

If you take the word *imagination* apart, you will discover that it means merely the postulating of images or the assembly of perceptions into creations as you desire them. Imagination is something one does of his free will. Delusion could be said to be something forced upon one by his aberrations. All one has to know about imagination is know when he is imagining and when he is not.

Valences

You may have noticed, as you were perceiving   195
things which have occurred in the past, that you were sometimes
apparently inside your own body and sometimes may have been
observing yourself. There are people who are never out of their own
body in recall and people who are never in it. There are many
valences in everyone. By a valence is meant an actual or a shadow
personality. One's own valence is his actual personality. Be assured,
however, he can get into a confusion with other bodies and persons.
If one is in one's own valence when he is recalling things, he sees
what he has seen just as though he were looking at it again with his
own eyes. This is a very desirable condition of affairs. The symptom
of being out of one's own valence and in a shadow valence might be
said to mean that one finds his own body too dangerous to occupy in
thought. Being out of valence makes perceptions hard to contact in
recall. You will find, as you continue these lists, repeating each one
over and over, that it becomes easier and easier to see things again
out of one's own eyes.

In the following list of questions and in any recall, one
should make an effort to take the viewpoint of himself, which is to
say, to see the scene and get the perceptions as he himself got them at
the time.

Can you recall a time when:

1. You watched a person you didn't like doing something you liked to do.

2. You saw a person you liked doing something you didn't like to do.

3. You watched a person you liked doing something you liked to do.

196

☐ Sight
☐ Smell
☐ Touch
☐ Color
☐ Tone
☐ External Motion
☐ Emotion
☐ Loudness
☐ Body Position
☐ Sound
☐ Weight
☐ Personal Motion

4. You saw a person you disliked doing something you disliked to do.

5. You noticed somebody wearing something you wore.

6. You found somebody using a mannerism you used.

7. You adopted a mannerism.

8. You found yourself and a dog being treated alike.

9. You made faces at yourself in the mirror.

10. You decided to be completely different from a person.

11. You discovered you were like an object.

12. You were classified[1] with an unfavorable person.

13. You were classified with a favorable person.

---

1.   classify: 1. to arrange or organize by classes; order according to class.

14. You found yourself dressed like many others.

15. You found you were different from somebody after all.

16. You noticed the difference between yourself and others.

17. You ate with somebody you liked.

18. You met a person who reminded you of another and noticed the difference between them.

19. You walked in step with somebody you liked.

20. You rode with somebody you admired.

21. You had to take the same position as somebody else.

22. You played a game with people you liked.

23. You found yourself doing something because somebody in your early youth did it.

24. You found yourself refusing to do something because somebody in your early youth did it.

□ *Sight*
□ *Smell*
□ *Touch*
□ *Color*
□ *Tone*
□ *External Motion*
□ *Emotion*
□ *Loudness*
□ *Body Position*
□ *Sound*
□ *Weight*
□ *Personal Motion*

Note that the word *like* is used to mean *admire* or feel affection for and also to be similar to. The effort of valences could be said to mean trying to be like one's friends and unlike one's enemies. Unfortunately in life one often has comparisons and similarities between himself and his enemies and has dissimilarities pointed out between himself and his friends. The adjustment of this is desirable so that one feels free to follow through any motion or action of any human being without associating the motion or action with either friend or enemy.

As an effort to straighten out one's associations and dis-associations regarding people, the following questions are appended as the second part of List Nine.

198

Recall:

☐ Sight
☐ Smell
☐ Touch
☐ Color
☐ Tone
☐ External Motion
☐ Emotion
☐ Loudness
☐ Body Position
☐ Sound
☐ Weight
☐ Personal Motion

1. A person who looks like you.

2. A person who has physical troubles similar to yours.

3. A person from whom you got a particular mannerism.

4. A person who reminds you of an animal you knew.

5. A person who compared you unfavorably to unfavorable persons.

6. A person who compared you favorably to favorable persons.

7. Two people whom you had confused with each other.

8. A person you knew long ago like a person you are living with.

9. A person whom you knew earlier who reminds you of a person with whom you are now connected.

10. Who you are most like. Who said so?

11. Who used to be afraid of sentiment?

12. Who didn't like to eat?

☐ Sight
☐ Smell
☐ Touch
☐ Color
☐ Tone
☐ External Motion
☐ Emotion
☐ Loudness
☐ Body Position
☐ Sound
☐ Weight
☐ Personal Motion

13. Who was never supposed to amount to anything?

14. Who associated with people too much?

15. Who made life miserable for everybody?

16. Who had bad manners?

17. Who did you know earlier that had the pain that bothers you?

18. Who would you most want to be like?

19. Who would you most hate to be like?

20. Who held[2] that you amounted to nothing?

21. Who tried to keep you in line?

22. Who flattered you?

23. Who fed you?

199

It would be a good idea to go back over the last half of List Nine and recall specific incidents with all possible perceptions which illustrate the answers to these questions.

___

2.   hold: 12. to believe, to consider, to assert.

200

Interruptions

Slowness or uncertainty of speech, stage fright in part, slowness of computation, which is to say thinking, and hesitancy in taking directions stem mainly from being interrupted in physical actions during early youth.

The child, because he may bring danger upon himself, is continually interrupted in his physical actions. He reaches for something and is turned away from it, not simply by words, but by being himself removed from the object or having the object removed from him. He is kept out of spaces he wishes to enter by being pulled back. He is given one thing when he wants another. His self-determinism is continually interrupted thus in his efforts to explore, obtain or get rid of matter, energy, space or time. From these early interruptions the child builds up a long chain of experiences of interruption, not simply by speech but by barriers and obstacles in the physical universe. If he has not been thoroughly interrupted when a child, he can analytically assess later interruptions, but if he has been handled and denied so as to interrupt him when he is young, his power of decision is inhibited, to say nothing of his power of speech and thought.

Recalling special incidents as requested in this list brings them into the light and takes the power from these chains[1] of interruptions.

201

---

1.   chain: incidents of similar nature strung out in time; a series of incidents of similar nature or similar subject matter.

Can you recall a time when:

202

☐ *Sight*
☐ *Smell*
☐ *Touch*
☐ *Color*
☐ *Tone*
☐ *External Motion*
☐ *Emotion*
☐ *Loudness*
☐ *Body Position*
☐ *Sound*
☐ *Weight*
☐ *Personal Motion*

1. An object resisted you and you overcame it.

2. You couldn't move and then succeeded in getting away.

3. Somebody took something out of your hands and finished it.

4. Your physical action was interrupted.

5. A machine did not start.

6. Somebody jumped at you unexpectedly.

7. You were told a ghost story.

8. You had to give up a career.

9. Somebody touched your mouth.

10. You tried to raise your hand and were blocked.

11. You found the road was closed.

12. You couldn't get something into something.

13. You were halted by a friend.

14. Your father showed you how it was really done.

15. Somebody made you take care of something.

16. It was demonstrated you were putting it to the wrong use.

17. You were corrected "for your own good."

18. You knew somebody who had a mania[2] for using only the right word.

19. You were "helped" by having your sentence finished.

☐ Sight
☐ Smell
☐ Touch
☐ Color
☐ Tone
☐ External Motion
☐ Emotion
☐ Loudness
☐ Body Position
☐ Sound
☐ Weight
☐ Personal Motion

203

20. You couldn't go at the last minute.

21. You knew somebody who corrected the words you used for songs.

22. You weren't permitted to cry.

23. Noise got on somebody's nerves.

24. You couldn't finish it for want of time.

25. You had to be patient.

26. You couldn't go just then.

27. You were going but you were stopped.

28. Somebody tried to stop you but you kept on anyway.

29. You used it just as you pleased.

30. You had not been halted.

31. You got loose and continued.

32. You yelled anyway.

33. You completed it despite somebody.

---

2.   mania: 1. excessive excitement or enthusiasm.

34. You had to stop bolting[3] your food.

35. You drank all you pleased.

36. You weren't supposed to fight.

37. Somebody checked[4] a muscular reaction.

38. You were very enthusiastic and somebody cooled it quickly.

39. You went on in spite of weariness.

40. You broke a habit.

41. You found somebody wasn't as strong as you had supposed.

42. You discovered you could have it after all.

43. You found the real motive was selfishness.

44. You got out from under domination.

45. You discovered it wasn't for your own good after all.

46. You stopped yourself from interrupting somebody.

47. You found other people weren't wiser than you.

48. Everybody thought you were wrong but discovered you had been right.

49. You attained the goal anyway.

204

☐ Sight
☐ Smell
☐ Touch
☐ Color
☐ Tone
☐ External Motion
☐ Emotion
☐ Loudness
☐ Body Position
☐ Sound
☐ Weight
☐ Personal Motion

---

3.   bolt: 3. to gulp down (food) hastily.
4.   check: 2. to make a sudden stop.

50. You discovered another person wasn't worth having.

51. You restrained an urge to destroy something.

52. You disobeyed the law and got away with it.

53. Lightning didn't strike you.

54. You fixed something.

55. You ignored an interruption to your reading.

□ *Sight*

□ *Smell*

□ *Touch*

□ *Color*

□ *Tone*

□ *External Motion*

□ *Emotion*

□ *Loudness*

□ *Body Position*

□ *Sound*

□ *Weight*

□ *Personal Motion*

205

206

Invalidation Section

Aberrated individuals use two distinct and very   207
aberrated methods of controlling others. The first consists of forcing
the other person to do exactly what is desired with the mechanism of
recrimination[1] and denial of friendship or support unless instant
compliance takes place. In other words, "You do exactly what I say or
I am no ally of yours." This is outright domination. Additionally,
it seeks by anger and outright criticism, accusations, and other
mechanisms to pound another individual into submission by making
him less. The second method might be called domination by nullification. This is covert and quite often the person upon whom it
is exerted remains unsuspecting beyond the fact that he knows he is
very unhappy. This is the coward's method of domination. The
person using it feels that he is less than the individual upon whom he
is using it and has not the honesty or fortitude[2] to admit the fact to
himself. He then begins, much as termites gnaw away a foundation,
as in California, to pull the other individual "down to size," using
small carping criticisms. The one who is seeking to dominate strikes
heavily at the point of pride and capability of his target and yet, if at
any moment the target challenges the nullifier, the person using
the mechanism claims he is doing so solely out of assistance and
friendship, or disavows completely that it has been done. Of the two
methods, the latter is far more damaging. A person using this method
seeks to reduce another individual down to a point where he can be
completely controlled and will not stop until he has reduced the
target into a confused apathy. The lowest common denominator of
nullification could be called "invalidation." The nullifier seeks to
invalidate not only the person but the skills and knowledge of his
target. The possessions of the target are said to be not quite as
important as they might be. The experiences of the person being

1.   recrimination: 2. a counter charge.
2.   fortitude: courage in bearing pain or trouble.

nullified are minimized. The target's looks, strength, physical capabilities and potentialities are also invalidated. All this may be done so covertly that it appears to be "in the best interest of" the target. The nullifier seeks to "improve" the person being invalidated.

The first question of this list should be, of course, how many people have you known who have sought consistently under the mask of seeking to aid you to tear you apart as a person, and reduce your future, your hopes, your goals, and the very energy of your life?

208

Can you recall a time when:

☐ *Sight*
☐ *Smell*
☐ *Touch*
☐ *Color*
☐ *Tone*
☐ *External Motion*
☐ *Emotion*
☐ *Loudness*
☐ *Body Position*
☐ *Sound*
☐ *Weight*
☐ *Personal Motion*

1. A person much smaller than you resented your size.

2. A person bigger than you made you feel inferior.

3. A person would not let you finish something.

4. An object was too much for you.

5. You found a space too big.

6. You were pushed back because you were too small.

7. You didn't make the team.

8. You found you were adequate.

9. You found somebody had lied about how bad you were.

10. You discovered you had been right after all.

11. You found your decision would have been best.

12. You solved a problem nobody else could do.

13. You discovered there were homelier people in the world than you.

14. You found you could ignore somebody's opinion.

☐ Sight
☐ Smell
☐ Touch
☐ Color
☐ Tone
☐ External Motion
☐ Emotion
☐ Loudness
☐ Body Position
☐ Sound
☐ Weight
☐ Personal Motion

209

15. You found somebody else thought you really had done something good.

16. You were admired for your looks.

17. You overcame a machine.

18. You accomplished an arduous[3] journey.

19. You discovered somebody who slurred[4] you was dishonest in other ways.

20. You found you were bigger and more powerful than an animal.

21. You discovered your competence.

22. You bested somebody thoroughly.

23. An enemy cried for quarter.[5]

24. You drew blood on somebody else.

25. You took the lion's share[6] and kept it.

26. You made your weight felt.

---

3.   arduous: needing much effort, laborious.
4.   slur: 4. to speak ill of.
5.   quarter: 9. mercy toward an enemy or opponent.
6.   lion's share: the largest share; an unreasonably large portion.

27. You were too heavy for somebody.

28. You killed something.

29. You won.

30. You were able to get away from somebody who invalidated you.

31. You discovered you were right and the old man was wrong.

32. You found you could get better.

33. You got well when they had no hope for you.

34. You surprised yourself with your own endurance.

35. You discovered you did understand.

36. You did a job nobody believed possible.

37. You were proud of yourself today.

210

☐ Sight
☐ Smell
☐ Touch
☐ Color
☐ Tone
☐ External Motion
☐ Emotion
☐ Loudness
☐ Body Position
☐ Sound
☐ Weight
☐ Personal Motion

The Elements

Man's primary foe in his environment is the   211
weather. Houses, stoves, clothes, and even food, in the degree that it
furnishes body warmth and mobility, are weapons of defense against
storm, cold, heat and night.

Can you recall a time when:

☐ *Sight*
☐ *Smell*
☐ *Touch*
☐ *Color*
☐ *Tone*
☐ *External Motion*
☐ *Emotion*
☐ *Loudness*
☐ *Body Position*
☐ *Sound*
☐ *Weight*
☐ *Personal Motion*

1. You bested a storm.

2. You enjoyed thunder.

3. You had fun in snow.

4. You enjoyed the sunshine.

5. Everyone else said it was too hot but you enjoyed it.

6. You bested an area of water.

7. The rain was soothing.

8. You were glad it was a cloudy day.

9. The wind excited you.

10. The night was soft.

11. You were glad to see the sun.

12. The weather was friendly.

13. You bested some surf.

14. The air was exhilarating.

15. You were glad of the season.

212

☐ Sight
☐ Smell
☐ Touch
☐ Color
☐ Tone
☐ External
Motion
☐ Emotion
☐ Loudness
☐ Body
Position
☐ Sound
☐ Weight
☐ Personal
Motion

16. You got warm after being too cold.

17. A dawn excited you.

18. You felt you owned the stars.

19. You were excited over a hailstone.

20. You discovered the pattern of snowflakes.

21. The dew was bright.

22. A soft fog rolled.

23. You won over a storm's violence.

24. It was terrible outside and you were snug in your house.

25. The wind felt good.

26. You lived through it.

27. You discovered you liked your own climate.

28. You were glad to see spring.

29. You felt you could best the winds of the world.

30. You admired a storm.

31. You enjoyed lightning.

Begin at List One again and go through all lists once more until book has been used many times.

213

214

Special Session Lists

If Recalling a Certain Thing
Made You Uncomfortable

215

It may be, as you recall certain incidents in your life, that you are rendered uncomfortable. There are several ways of overcoming this. If actual physical pain is part of the situation you have recalled, do not try to force yourself further into it, but concentrate on later incidents which gradually get you back up to present time. These questions will assist you to do that.

☐ *Sight*
☐ *Smell*
☐ *Touch*
☐ *Color*
☐ *Tone*
☐ *External Motion*
☐ *Emotion*
☐ *Loudness*
☐ *Body Position*
☐ *Sound*
☐ *Weight*
☐ *Personal Motion*

1. Recall a pleasant incident which happened later.

2. Recall what you were doing this time last year.

3. Recall a moment when you were really enjoying yourself.

4. Recall what you were doing this time last month.

5. Recall what you were doing yesterday.

6. Recall something pleasant that happened today.

Recall all these things consecutively once again.

If no physical pain was included but sorrow was, recall the following:

216

☐ *Sight*
☐ *Smell*
☐ *Touch*
☐ *Color*
☐ *Tone*
☐ *External Motion*
☐ *Emotion*
☐ *Loudness*
☐ *Body Position*
☐ *Sound*
☐ *Weight*
☐ *Personal Motion*

1. The next time after that you acquired something you liked.

2. Recall something you have now which you enjoy.

3. Recall something you wanted a long time and finally got.

4. Recall the time somebody was very nice to you.

5. Recall the last money you got.

6. Recall eating dinner last night.

7. Recall eating today.

Recall all of these incidents over again with all available perceptics.

If you consistently hit physical pain and grief incidents in your processing and do not seem to be able to do anything about it, call your local Dianetic auditor and arrange a professional visit so that you can be brought up to a point where the list is a benefit.

If you merely became uncomfortable without great sorrow or physical pain, but simply wanted to avoid the recollection, use the following list:

1. Recall the incident again in its entirety from first to last.

2. Recall the incident once more.

3. Recall an earlier incident similar to it.

4. Recall an even earlier incident similar to it.

☐ Sight

☐ Smell

☐ Touch

☐ Color

☐ Tone

☐ External Motion

☐ Emotion

☐ Loudness

☐ Body Position

☐ Sound

☐ Weight

☐ Personal Motion

5. Recall the earliest incident that you can get like it.

6. Recall all these incidents, one after the other, in their entirety.

7. Recall all the incidents again, one after the other, from the earliest to the latest.

8. Recall all these incidents again.

9. Go over the chain of similar incidents and find later ones on up to present time.

10. Recall a pleasant incident which has happened in the last few days. Get all possible perceptics on it.

11. Recall what you were doing an hour ago.

This usually stabilizes any of the above conditions.

1. Recall a time which really seems real to you.

2. Recall a time when you felt real affinity[1] from someone.

3. Recall a time when someone was in good communication with you.

4. Recall a time when you felt deep affinity for somebody else.

218

□ *Sight*
□ *Smell*
□ *Touch*
□ *Color*
□ *Tone*
□ *External Motion*
□ *Emotion*
□ *Loudness*
□ *Body Position*
□ *Sound*
□ *Weight*
□ *Personal Motion*

5. Recall a time when you knew you were really communicating to somebody.

6. Recall a time when several people agreed with you completely.

7. Recall a time when you were in agreement with somebody else.

8. Recall a time within the last two days when you felt affectionate.

9. Recall a time in the last two days when somebody felt affection for you.

10. Recall a time in the last two days when you were in good communication with someone.

11. Recall a time in the last two days which really seems real to you.

12. Recall a time in the last two days when you were in good communication with people.

Recall several incidents of each kind.

---

1.   affinity: the feeling of love or liking for something or someone.

According to the practice of medicine and after experiment, it has been found that B_1 is necessary in large amounts during processing. A good protein diet and some 100 to 200 mg. per day of B_1 have been found to materially assist processing. Failure to take B_1 and to use a heavy protein diet have been found to result in nightmares and nervousness when one is undergoing processing. Note that this is a medical finding dating back many years and is not original with Dianetics.

219

End of Session List

Each time you give yourself a session of processing you should finish off with the following routine without disc.

1. Rapidly sketch[2] over the session just ended.

2. Sketch over what you have been doing again, with particular attention to how you have been sitting.

3. Go over the period of the session with regard only to what you have been doing with your hands and things in the exterior world you have heard during this session.

4. Fix your attention upon a pleasant object near you now.

Repeat this until you feel refreshed in your immediate surroundings.

---

2.   sketch: go over mentally.

220

About the Author

Whether introduced through the pages of one of his 589 published works, or through a direct personal encounter, L. Ron Hubbard is a man once met, never forgotten. And while he has become known for advances in a variety of fields, he is known by millions as one of the foremost writers of self-betterment books in the world today. His works on the subjects of Dianetics, human relationships and life itself have sold over 23 million copies.

Ron's hallmark is that he writes with a purpose, reads insatiably, researches meticulously and lives what he writes about. Few are the writers that can appeal so well to so many with a first-hand knowledge of the basics of life and ability.

Born in Tilden, Nebraska on March 13, 1911, Ron spent his early years in Montana where he learned horsemanship, growing up with the last of the old frontiersmen and cowboys. An old Indian medicine man was a best friend.

The son of a naval man, L. Ron Hubbard traveled with his parents to China, Japan, and the Pacific Islands. At only fifteen years of age, he traveled far on his own into China and to Manchuria, encountering wide variations in culture and custom in the peoples he met.

After returning to the United States, Ron completed his schooling and supported himself while in college and in his research by writing a wide variety of articles and stories. His perception of life quickly gained him acclaim as he poured out literally millions of words. He wrote aviation articles (he was also a glider pilot and barnstormer), westerns, sports stories, sea stories, detective thrillers, military intrigues and adventure of every kind on every continent. Later he joined forces with one of the greatest editors of science fiction, John W. Campbell, Jr., and helped to launch what was later called "The Golden Age of Science Fiction."

In 1932, Hubbard was startled to find that the culture in which we live had no more workable knowledge of the mind than a shaman of the Goldi people of Manchuria or a Blackfoot medicine man. Here was a society that was excelling in the physical sciences but had no means of bettering man's ability to live his life and secure his own sanity.

222

Between the years of 1933 and 1940, Hubbard conducted three expeditions that in 1940 earned him election to the prestigious Explorer's Club of New York.

Deeply affected by his service in the Second World War, Ron continued his research. He began to synthesize what he had learned of Eastern philosophy, nuclear physics and scientific methodology, and working with men in war.

Ron made breakthroughs and developed techniques that enabled his own recovery from his war experiences. He concluded that the results he was obtaining could help others to gain greater ability, health and happiness and it was during this period that the basic tenets of Dianetics were formed.

In 1948, L. Ron Hubbard had written what was later titled *Dianetics: The Original Thesis*. This manuscript summarized his research and delineated the principles he had proven. Passed from hand to hand in professional circles, it soon warranted the publication of a book on the subject.

Dianetics: The Modern Science of Mental Health was then published in May 1950. Response to the book was positive and instantaneous. By late summer 1950, the book was high on the New York Times Best Seller lists. People across the United States were reading the book and using the techniques outlined in the book to attain new levels of certainty and ability.

L. Ron Hubbard had little respect for the "official" treatments employed in the name of "mental health." And so he became a target for those who supported programs of psychosurgery, electric shock, drugs and hypnosis.

Undaunted, his research continued and still continues today.

Since those early days, L. Ron Hubbard has continued his research and written over 50 works on the subjects of philosophy, human relationships and self-betterment. He has also delivered about 3,000 hours of lectures containing an estimated 25,000,000 words on these subjects. These works represent a complete, fully detailed and workable technology of the mind and life.

223

Self Analysis is, in itself, a breakthrough. With this book a person can gain the benefits of the vast technology that now exists on the mind without having to become a technical expert or even leaving one's home.

With this technology it has become possible for men to truly become sane and confident in their abilities and handling of life.

L. Ron Hubbard's research and discoveries and his technology of Dianetics have improved the lives of millions.

People all over the world consider they have no truer friend. □

224

Glossary

Words of the English language that are defined in this
glossary have an abbreviation at the end of the definition that
indicates the source dictionary of that particular definition. These are
designated as follows:

AHD — *American Heritage Dictionary*
CHD — *Computer Handbook and Dictionary*
NCD — *The New Century Dictionary*
OAD — *Oxford American Dictionary*
OED — *Oxford English Dictionary* (2-volume compact edition)
RHCD — *Random House College Dictionary*
RHDEL — *Random House Dictionary of the English Language*
SDCIP — *Standard Dictionary of Computers and Information Processing*
WNWD — *Webster's New World Dictionary*
WTNID — *Webster's Third New International Dictionary*

225

Words of Dianetics that are footnoted have definitions
developed by the author in his researches. They are not followed by
any abbreviations.

The numbers that appear in parentheses directly following
the entry words of each definition indicate the page number where
the word first appears in the text. The next number in a definition
will be the number of that definition in the dictionary it was
extracted from. It indicates that there are more definitions than are
listed here.

a aberration: (9) a departure from rational thought or behavior. From the Latin, *aberrare*, to wander from; Latin, *ab*, away, *errare*, to wander. It means basically to err, to make mistakes, or more specifically to have fixed ideas which are not true. The word is also used in its scientific sense. It means departure from a straight line. If a line should go from A to B, then if it is "aberrated" it would go from A to some other point, to some other point, to some other point, to some other point, to some other point and finally arrive at B. Taken in its scientific sense, it would also mean the lack of straightness or to see crookedly as, in example, a man sees a horse but thinks he sees an elephant. Aberrated conduct would be wrong conduct, or conduct not supported by reason. When a person has engrams, these tend to deflect what would be his normal ability to perceive truth and bring about an aberrated view of situations which then would cause an aberrated reaction to them. Aberration is opposed to sanity which would be its opposite.

acquaintance: (9) 3. personal knowledge. —*RHCD*

acute: (35) 4. (of disease) brief and severe. —*RHCD*

adorn(ed): (176) 1a. to make pleasing or attractive. —*WTNID*

adroit: (76) skillful, ingenious. —*OAD*

advance(d): (176) 2. to raise in rank or position: promote. —*WTNID*

agile: (78) nimble, quick-moving. —*OAD*

affinity: (218) the feeling of love or liking for something or someone. Affinity is a phenomena of space in that it expresses the willingness to occupy the same place as the thing which is loved or liked. The reverse of it would be antipathy, "dislike" or rejection which would be the unwillingness to occupy the same space as or the unwillingness to approach something or someone. It came from the French, *affinite*, affinity, kindred, alliance, nearness and also from the Latin, *affinis*, meaning near, bordering upon.

ally: (23) 2. to associate or connect by some mutual relationship. —*RHCD*

amiable: (106) feeling and inspiring friendliness, good-tempered. —*OAD*

analytical: (61) capable of resolving, such as problems, situations. The word *analytical* is from the Greek *analysis* meaning resolve, undo, loosen, which is to say take something to pieces to see what it is made of. This is one of those examples of the shortcomings of the English language since no dictionary gives the word *analytical* any connection with thinking, reasoning, perceiving, which in essence is what it would have to mean, even in English.

animate: (21) 1. to give life to; make alive. —*WNWD*

annihilate(-tion): (151) 1. to destroy completely; put out of existence; demolish. —*WNWD*

antipathy: (100) 1. a strong or deep-rooted dislike. —*WNWD*

appoint(ed): (140) 1. to fix or decide by authority. —*OAD*

appreciate: (34) 3. to understand. —*OAD*

apprehension: (91) 1. a feeling of fear about a **b** possible danger or difficulty. —*OAD*

approximation: (143) 3. a coming or getting near to identity in quantity, quality or degree; an approach to a correct estimate or conception of anything. —*OED*

ardent: (ix) full of ardor (great warmth of feeling), enthusiastic. —*OAD*

arduous: (209) needing much effort, laborious. —*OAD*

arrest(ed): (155) 2. to attract and hold. —*RHCD*

artful(ly): (46) 1. crafty; cunning; tricky. —*RHCD*

arthritis: (5) a condition causing inflammation, pain and stiffness in the joints. —*OAD*

assail(ed): (155) 1. to set upon with violence; assault. —*RHCD*

atomic physics: (9) nuclear physics: the branch of physics that deals with the behavior, structure, and component parts of atomic nuclei (plural of *nucleus*, 5. the positively charged mass within an atom, composed of neutrons and protons, and possessing most of the mass but occupying only a small fraction of the volume of the atom). —*RHCD*

attend: (15) 3. to take care of or wait upon; minister to. —*RHCD*

attendant: (20) 3. accompanying as a circumstance or result. —*WNWD*

auditor: (3) the individual who administers Dianetic procedures. To audit means "to listen" and also "to compute."

authoritarian: (46) favoring complete obedience to authority as opposed to individual freedom. —*OAD*

avert(ed): (115) 2. to prevent, to ward off. —*OAD*

avid(ly): (100) 2. eager and enthusiastic. —*WNWD*

avow(edly): (45) to admit, to declare openly. —*OAD*

awareness: (19) the ability to perceive the existence of.

axioms: (64) statements of natural laws on the order of those of the physical sciences.

basic: (64) the first experience recorded in mental image pictures of that type of pain, sensation, discomfort, etc. Every chain (a series of incidents of similar nature or similar subject matter) has its basic. It is a peculiarity and a fact that when one gets down to the basic on a chain (a) it erases and (b) the whole chain vanishes for good. Basic is simply earliest.

behold(ing): (151) to see, to observe. —*OAD*

best(ed): (74) to defeat, to outdo, to outwit. —*OAD*

biologist: (22) an expert in biology (the scientific study of life and structure of living things). —*OAD*

blatant: (46) very bad, obvious. —*ed.*

blunder(ing): (18) 2. to move or act blindly, stupidly, or without direction or steady guidance. —*RHDEL*

b **blunt(ed):** (24) 3. to make less effective. —*WNWD*

bolt(ing): (204) 3. to gulp down (food) hastily. —*OAD*

breast(ing): (18) 2. to face or meet firmly; move forward against. —*WNWD*

bushel: (14) a measure for grain and fruit (32 quarts). —*OAD*

cabal: (47) 1. a secret plot. —*OAD*

caliber: (37) 3. ability, importance. —*OAD*

capricious: (48) characterized by or subject to whim; impulsive and unpredictable. —*AHD*

carp(ing): (27) to keep finding fault, to raise petty objections. —*OAD*

case opening: (63) in starting a case we can say that we are trying to free all possible attention units (a theta energy quantity of awareness existing in the mind in varying quantity from person to person) as fast as possible.

cast: (3) 54. a slight tinge of some color; hue; shade. —*RHCD*

catalyze: (104) to act upon by catalysis (the causing or accelerating of a chemical change by the addition of a substance that is not permanently affected by the reaction). —*RHCD*

central nervous system: (99) the brain and the spinal cord. —*OAD*

chain(s): (201) incidents of similar nature strung out in time; a series of incidents of similar nature or similar subject matter.

charge: (65) stored energy or stored recreatable potentials of energy.

charitable: (34) 2. kindly or lenient in judging people, acts, etc. —*RHCD*

check(ed): (204) 2. to make a sudden stop. —*OAD*

chemistry: (22) 1. the scientific study of substances and their elements and of how they react when combined or in contact with one another. —*OAD*

Christendom: (xiv) all Christians, Christian countries. —*OAD*

chronic: (33) 1. affecting a person for a long time. —*OAD*

citadel(s): (ix) a fortress overlooking a city. —*OAD*

classify(-fied): (196) 1. to arrange or organize by classes; order according to class. —*RHCD*

Clear: (48) an unaberrated person. He is rational in that he forms the best possible solutions he can on the data he has and from his viewpoint. He obtains the maximum pleasure for the organism, present and future, as well as for the subjects along the other dynamics.

clearing: (64) what is clearing but regaining awareness that one is himself and regaining confidence.

cloud(ed): (3) 11. to overshadow; obscure; darken. —*RHCD*

coal heaver: (10) a man employed in loading or unloading coal from ships. —*ed.*

co-auditing: (38) is an abbreviation for cooperative auditing. It means a team of any two

people who are helping each other reach a better life.

collective (state): (15) 5. organized according to the principles of collectivism (the political principle of centralized social and economic control, especially of all means of production). —*RHCD*

commit(ted): (159) 3c. to expose to risk or danger. —*WTNID*

communist(ic): (45) 1. an advocate of communism (2. a system of social organization in which all economic and social activity is controlled by a totalitarian state dominated by a single and self-perpetuating political party). —*RHCD*

concede(d): (143) 1. to acknowledge as true, just or proper; admit. —*RHCD*

conceive: (125) 3. to hold as an opinion; think; believe. —*RHCD*

concept: (20) that which is retained after something has been perceived.

confound(ed): (160) 1. to perplex or amaze; confuse. —*RHCD*

conjurer(s): (10) 2. a magician; sorcerer. —*WNWD*

connotation: (134) the implied meaning of an expression in addition to its primary meaning. —*OAD*

consciousness: (17) awareness of now.

conservation: (131) 1. the act of conserving; preservation from loss, injury, decay or waste. —*RHCD*

constancy: (45) 2. faithfulness. —*OAD*

contain: (160) 4. to keep under proper control; restrain. —*RHCD*

contortionist: (128) a performer who can twist his body into unusual postures. —*OAD*

contrary: (117) 4. inclined to oppose or disagree stubbornly. —*WNWD*

coolie(s): (10) an unskilled native laborer in the Far East. —*OAD*

court(ing): (160) 15. to seek the affections of. —*RHCD*

cover: a commanding position with regard to. —*ed.*

covert hostility: (104) here is the person who hates but is afraid to say he hates, who deals in treachery and who yet expects to be forgiven.

criterion: (27) a standard of judgment. —*OAD*

cunning: (22) 3. made or done with skill or ingenuity. —*WNWD*

cynical: (xiv) 1. believing that people are motivated in all their actions only by selfishness; denying the sincerity of people's motives and actions or the value of living. —*WNWD*

dear: (103) 1. much loved; beloved. —*WNWD*

defeatist: (31) a person who expects to be defeated or accepts defeat too easily. —*OAD*

demarcation: (17) 3. a separation or distinction. —*WNWD*

demise: (51) death. —*OAD*

democratic: (45) 2. in accordance with the principle of equal rights for all. —*OAD*

d

227

d **depository:** (44) having to do with matter collected in any part of any organism. —*ed.*

depreciate: (135) 5. to decline in value. —*RHCD*

derivation(s): (144) 3. the source from which something is derived; origin. —*RHCD*

dermatitis: (31) inflammation of the skin. —*OAD*

desensitize: (63) to make less sensitive to a substance or influence. —*OAD*

detail(s): (46) 1. to give particulars of, to describe fully. —*OAD*

detriment: (134) 1. loss, damage, disadvantage, or injury. —*RHCD*

devaluate: (47) 1. to deprive of value; reduce the value of. —*RHCD*

diabetes: (105) a disease in which sugar and starch are not properly absorbed by the body. —*OAD*

diabolical: (10) 2. fiendishly clever or cunning or annoying. —*OAD*

Dianetics: (ix) Dianetics spiritual healing technology. The word is from the Greek, *dia,* through, and *nous,* soul. It is a very exact analytical approach to the mind.

differentiate(-tion): (48) 3. to perceive the difference in or between. —*RHCD*

disabuse: (6) to disillusion (to set free from pleasant but mistaken beliefs), to free from a false idea. —*OAD*

discharged: (31) erased.

discordant: (91) 2. disagreeable to the ear; harsh. —*RHCD*

disperse(d): (111) to scatter, to go or drive or send in different directions. —*OAD*

dissipate(-ting): (70) 1. to break up and scatter; dispel; disperse. —*WNWD*

dregs: (132) 3. a small amount remaining; residue. —*WNWD*

dynamic: (13) 1. relating to energy or physical force in motion. —*WNWD*

dynamics: (48) in Dianetics, survival is understood to be the basic single thrust of life through time and space, energy and matter. Survival is subdivided into eight dynamics. Man does not survive for self alone, nor yet for sex, nor yet for groups, nor yet only for the species of man. Man apparently survives, as do other living organisms, along eight separate channels. These channels are called the dynamics, and these eight represent the eight fundamental urges or drives which motivate conduct.

The *first dynamic* is the urge toward survival of self.

The *second dynamic* is the urge toward survival through sex or children. This dynamic actually has two divisions. Second dynamic (a) is the sexual act itself and second dynamic (b) is the family unit, including the rearing of children.

The *third dynamic* is the urge toward survival through a group of individuals or as a group. Any group or part of an entire class could be considered to be part of the third dynamic. The school, the club, the team, the town, the nation are examples of groups.

228

The *fourth dynamic* is the urge toward survival through all mankind and as all mankind.

The *fifth dynamic* is the urge toward survival through life forms such as animals, birds, insects, fish and vegetation, and is the urge to survive as these.

The *sixth dynamic* is the urge toward survival as the physical universe and has as its components matter, energy, space and time, from which we derive the word MEST.

The *seventh dynamic* is the urge toward survival through spirits or as a spirit. Anything spiritual, with or without identity, would come under the seventh dynamic. A subheading of this dynamic is ideas and concepts such as beauty, and the desire to survive through these.

The *eighth dynamic* is the urge toward survival through a Supreme Being, or more exactly, Infinity.

electric shock "therapy": (132) there is no therapeutic reason for shocking anyone and there are no authentic cases on record of anyone having been cured of anything by shock.

electron: (21) a particle of matter with a negative electric charge. —*OAD*

emotion: (35) emotion could be called the energy manifestation of affinity. As used in Dianetics, emotion could be called the index of the state of being. In the English language, "emotional" is often considered synonymous with "irrational." This would seem to assume that if one is emotional one cannot be reasonable. No more unreasonable assumption could possibly be made.

endearing: (94) 2. expressing affection. —*WNWD*

endeavor: (xii) an earnest attempt or effort.— *WNWD*

endocrine: (44) (of a gland) pouring its secretions straight into the blood, not through a duct. —*OAD*

engram: (7) a mental image picture which is a recording of a time of physical pain and unconsciousness. It must by definition have impact or injury as part of its content.

enlist(ing): (152) 4. to secure (a person, services, etc.) for some cause, enterprise, etc. —*RHCD*

enmity: (169) a feeling or condition of hostility; hatred; ill will; animosity; antagonism. —*RHCD*

entheta: (47) means enturbulated theta (thought or life); especially refers to communications, which, based on lies and confusions, are slanderous, choppy or destructive in an attempt to overwhelm or suppress a person or group.

enturbulate(s): (45) cause to be turbulent or agitated and disturbed.

environ: (45) surrounding area; vicinity. —*ed.*

eradicate: (31) 2. to get rid of; wipe out; destroy. —*WNWD*

esoteric: (15) 1b. beyond the understanding or knowledge of most people. —*WNWD*

e

e **ESP:** (66) extrasensory perception: perception or communication outside of normal sensory activity, as in telepathy and clairvoyance. —*RHCD*

ethics: (39) ethics are the actions an individual takes on himself in order to accomplish optimum survival for himself and others. Ethical conduct includes the adherence to the moral codes of the society in which we live.

evoke: (135) 1. to call up, produce or suggest (memories, feelings, etc.). —*RHCD*

existence: (10) an existing state or fact of being; life; living; continuance of being and occurrence; specific manifestation.

experience: (18) 1. actual observation of facts or events, activity or practice in doing something. —*OAD*

fascist: (26) 2. a person who believes in or practices fascism (2. a system of government characterized by rigid one-party dictatorship, forcible suppression of opposition, private economic enterprise under centralized governmental control, belligerent nationalism, racism, and militarism, etc.). —*WNWD*

fillet: (97) 6. a boneless, lean piece of meat or fish. —*WNWD*

flare: (6) 2a. to cause to flare (*n.* 3. a sudden outburst [as of sound, excitement, or anger]: *a flare of temper*). —*WTNID*

flighty: (48) 1. given to sudden whims; not taking things seriously. —*WNWD*

fortitude: (207) courage in bearing pain or trouble. —*OAD*

gala: (167) 1. festive; showy. —*RHCD*

gate, give (someone) the: (111) 12b. to dismiss from one's employ. —*RHCD*

gentleman with the scythe: (20) grim reaper: death, especially when personified as a man or skeleton with a scythe. —*WTNID*

gland(s): (19) an organ that secretes substances that are to be used by the body or expelled from it. —*OAD*

goal of life: (9) the goal of life can be considered to be infinite survival. Man, as a life form, can be demonstrated to obey in all his actions and purposes the one command: "Survive!"

graybeard(s): (18) an old man. —*WNWD*

groundless: (145) without reason or cause; unjustified. —*WNWD*

guidon: (ix) a small flag or pennant used as a military unit's standard. —*OAD*

haggard: (15) looking exhausted and ugly from prolonged worry or illness or lack of sleep. —*OAD*

harken: (xiv) 1. to listen; give heed or attend to what is said. —*RHCD*

hearsay evidence: (65) testimony given by a witness based on what he has heard from another person. —*RHCD*

hitherto: (28) until this time. —*OAD*

hold (held): (199) 12. to believe, to consider, to assert. —*OAD*

hormone: (105) 1. a substance formed in some organ of the body . . . [glands] and carried by a body fluid to another organ or tissue, where it has a specific effect: now often prepared synthetically. —*WNWD*

humor: (48) humor is rejection. The ability to reject. The ability to throw something away. That is humor.

hypnotism: (45) amnesia trance for the purpose of planting suggestions.

hypothyroid: (105) of, characterized by, or having hypothyroidism (1. deficient activity of the thyroid gland. 2. disorder resulting from this). —*WNWD*

IBM card: (3) a type of paper card that may have information recorded on it by means of punched holes, and which may be read by a computer. —*CHD*

ignominious(ly): (38) bringing contempt or disgrace, humiliating. —*OAD*

illuminate(d): (165) 4. to enlighten, as with knowledge. —*RHCD*

illusion(s): (19) any idea, space, energy, object or time concept which one creates himself.

immune: (44) 1. protected from a disease or the like. —*RHCD*

implant: (133) a painful and forceful means of overwhelming a being with artificial purpose or false concepts in a malicious attempt to control and suppress him.

impotence(-cy): (45) 2. complete failure or serious impairment of sexual power, especially in the male. —*RHCD*

in: (167) 10. with respect to. —*OAD*

incident: (59) an experience, simple or complex, related by the same subject, location, perception or people that takes place in a short and finite time period such as minutes, hours or days; also, mental image pictures of such experiences.

index: (3) 2. an ordered list of references to the contents of a larger body of data, such as a file or record, together with the keys or reference notations for identifying, locating, searching or retrieving the contents. —*SDCIP*

index: (4) 4. an indication or sign of something. —*OAD*

interdependent: (25) dependent on each other. —*OAD*

intimacy: (19) 2. a close, familiar, and usually affectionate or loving, personal relationship. —*RHCD*

invalidate(s): (47) invalidation (refuting or degrading or discrediting or denying something someone else considers to be fact).

irrationality: (105) the inability to get right answers from data.

knowledge: (19) by knowledge we mean assured belief, that which is known information, instruction; enlightenment, learning; practical skill. By knowledge we mean data, factors and whatever can be thought about or perceived.

knuckle under: (39) 8b. to submit, yield. —*RHCD*

k

229

l **lest:** (152) 1. in order that not, to avoid the risk of, *lest we forget.* —*OAD*

liberal: (45) 6. favoring or permitting freedom of action, especially with respect to matters of personal belief or expression. —*RHCD*

lion's share: (209) the largest share; an unreasonably large portion. —*RHCD*

livelihood: (139) means of living or of supporting life. —*WNWD*

lock(s): (64) a mental image picture of an incident where one was knowingly or unknowingly reminded of a secondary or engram. It does not itself contain a blow or a burn or impact and is not any major cause of misemotion. It does not contain unconsciousness. It may contain a feeling of pain or illness, etc., but is not itself the source of it. Example: one sees a cake, feels sick. This is a lock on an engram of being made sick by eating cake. The picture of seeing a cake and feeling sick is a lock on (is locked to) the incident (unseen at the moment) of getting sick eating cake. When one finds a lock it can be run like any other mental image picture.

malicious(ly): (141) feeling or showing or caused by malice (a desire to harm others or to tease). —*OAD*

mania: (203) 1. excessive excitement or enthusiasm. —*RHCD*

manifestation(s): (21) 2. the state of being manifested (readily perceived by the eye or the understanding; evident; obvious; apparent; plain). —*RHCD*

margin: (14) 3. an amount over and above the essential minimum. —*OAD*

mart(s): (9) 1. a market or trading center. —*WNWD*

mayhap: (18) perhaps; maybe. —*WNWD*

mind: (23) is the command post of operation and is constructed to resolve problems and pose problems related to survival and only to survival.

minion(s): (15) 2. a subordinate official, deputy or the like. —*WNWD*

misapprehend(-nsion): (125) to misunderstand. —*OAD*

misconstrue(d): (144) to misinterpret. —*OAD*

monocell: (21) an organism composed of a single cell. —*ed.*

moral: (46) simply, totally and only—of or concerned with the judgment of the goodness or badness of human action and character; pertaining to good and evil. Designed to teach goodness or correctness of character and behavior; instructive of what is good and bad.

morals: (14) 11. principles or habits with respect to right or wrong conduct. —*RHCD*

negate(-tion): (34) to nullify, to disprove. —*OAD*

neurology(-gical): (44) the medical science of the nervous system and its disorders. —*AHD*

neurotic: (27) a person who is mainly harmful to himself by reason of his aberrations, but not to the point of suicide.

New Yorker: (38) a literary magazine in New York containing book and theater criticism. —*ed.*

Niagara: (134) a torrent, or flood. —*WNWD*

nullify(-fied): (30) 3. to cancel out. —*WNWD*

oblige(d): (116) 2. to help or gratify by performing a small service. —*OAD*

occasion(ed): (85) to cause. —*OAD*

occluded: (66) memory not available for recall. Someone who is occluded has a poor memory and poor recalls of the past.

olfactory: (94) 1. of or pertaining to the sense of smell. —*RHCD*

outmoded: (26) 2. not acceptable by present standards; no longer usable; obsolete. —*RHCD*

palatable: (7) 2. pleasing or acceptable to the mind or feelings. —*RHCD*

pale: (3) 3. not bright or brilliant; dim. —*RHCD*

pancreas: (105) a large, elongated gland situated behind the stomach and secreting a digestive juice into the small intestine: groups of . . . cells in the gland produce the hormone insulin (a protein hormone which helps the body use sugar and other carbohydrates). —*WNWD*

passionate: (95) 3. resulting from, expressing, or tending to arouse strong feeling; intense. —*WNWD*

pennyweight(s): (32) a measure of weight equal to 1/20 of an ounce in troy weight (a system of weights used for precious metals and gems, where there are twelve ounces to a normal pound). —*ed.*

perceptics: (68) any sense messages such as sight, sound, smell, etc.

Persian: (10) of Persia (the ancient and now the alternative name of Iran) or its people or language. —*OAD*

personality: (26) the individual, the personality, is the awareness of awareness unit, and the awareness of awareness unit is the person.

pertain: (66) 3. to have reference or relevance; be related. —*WNWD*

physical universe: (21) the universe of matter, energy, space and time. It would be the universe of the planets, their rocks, rivers and oceans, the universe of stars and galaxies, the universe of burning suns and time. In this universe we would not include theta (Greek for thought or life or the spirit) as an integral portion, although theta obviously impinges upon it as life.

physics: (22) 1. the scientific study of the properties and interactions of matter and energy. —*OAD*

physiology: (35) 2. the organic processes or functions of an organism or any of its parts. —*RHCD*

pleasure: (23) the Dianetic definition of pleasure is that the organism tending toward survival obtains pleasure by survival actions and the seeking of survival goals.

plutonium: (32) a radioactive chemical element, used in nuclear weapons and reactors. —*OAD*

poker: (101) a stiff metal rod for poking a fire. —*OAD*

p

p **pose(d):** (34) 1. to place in a specific position. —*AHD*

pose(s): (24) 1. to examine by questioning, question, interrogate. —*OED*

positive suggestion: (49) suggestion by the operator to a hypnotized subject with the sole end of creating a changed mental condition in the subject by implantation of the suggestion alone. It is a transplantation of something in the hypnotist's mind into the patient's mind. The patient is then to believe it and take it as part of himself.

postulate: (11) to assume (a thing) to be true, especially as a basis for reasoning. —*OAD*

potion: (5) a liquid for drinking as a medicine or drug, etc. —*OAD*

preclear: (63) any person who has been entered into Dianetic processing.

present time: (49) the ground, sky, walls, objects and people of the immediate environment. In other words, the anatomy of present time is the anatomy of the room or area in which you are at the moment when you view it.

prevail(ed): (110) 1. to be victorious, to gain the mastery. —*OAD*

problem: (24) the definition of a problem is *intention versus intention* or two or more opposing or conflicting views on the same subject.

processing: (5) the principle of making an individual look at his own existence, and improve his ability to confront what he is and where he is.

procreate(-tion): (45) to bring (a living thing) into existence by the natural process of reproduction, to generate. —*OAD*

prodigious(ly): (119) 2. enormous. —*OAD*

promiscuous(-culty): (45) 2. having sexual relations with many people. —*OAD*

proton: (21) a particle of matter with a positive electric charge. —*OAD*

prove(d): (160) 10. to be found by trial or experience to be. —*RHCD*

proximity: (29) 1. nearness. —*OAD*

prudent: (14) showing carefulness and foresight, avoiding rashness. —*OAD*

pseudo-: (46) *prefix*, false, insincere. —*OAD*

psychosomatic illnesses: (4) illnesses which have a mental origin but which are nevertheless organic.

psychotherapy: (31) treatment of mental disorders by the use of psychological (1. of or affecting the mind or its workings) methods. —*OAD*

pungent: (95) 1. having a strong sharp taste or smell. —*OAD*

qualm(s): (182) 2. a sudden feeling of uneasiness or doubt; misgiving. —*WNWD*

quarter: (209) 9. mercy toward an enemy or opponent. —*OAD*

reality: (47) is fundamentally agreement. That which we agree to be real is real.

reason: (17) 3. the ability to think, form judgments, draw conclusions, etc. —*WNWD*

recall: (59) present-time remembering **s** something that happened in the past. It is not reexperiencing it, reliving it or rerunning it. Recall does not mean going back to when it happened. It simply means that you are in present time, thinking of, remembering, putting your attention on something that happened in the past—all done from present time.

recess: (147) 3. a temporary withdrawal from or halting of work, business, study, etc. —*WNWD*

recrimination: (207) 2. a counter charge. —*AHD*

refuge: (115) 1. shelter or protection from danger, trouble, etc. —*RHCD*

regiment(ation): (15) 4. to organize in a rigid system under strict discipline and control. —*WNWD*

Repetitive Straightwire: (70) Straightwire to one incident done over and over until the incident is desensitized.

restimulate(d)(-tion): (71) the reactivation of a past memory due to similar circumstances in the present approximating circumstances of the past.

resurgent(-nces): (26) rising or tending to rise again; reviving. —*RHDEL*

revelry: (93) boisterous (rough and noisy) festivity. —*RHCD*

rheumatism: (31) any of several diseases causing pain in the joints or muscles or fibrous tissue. —*OAD*

Russell, Charles M.: (5) 1864–1926. Artist, writer and cowboy famous for his paintings and stories of cowboy life. —*ed.*

sadism: (45) 1. sexual gratification gained through causing physical pain or humiliation. —*RHCD*

sage: (10) a profoundly wise man. —*OAD*

satiate(d): (107) 2. to satisfy to the full. —*RHCD*

savant: (7) a man of profound or extensive learning. —*RHCD*

scythe: (20) a tool with a long, single-edged blade set at an angle on a long, curved handle, used in cutting long grass, grain, etc., by hand. —*WNWD*

secondary: (63) a mental image picture of a moment of severe and shocking loss or threat of loss which contains unpleasant emotion such as anger, fear, grief, apathy or "deathfulness." It is a mental image recording of a time of severe mental stress. A secondary is called a secondary because it itself depends upon an earlier engram with similar data but real pain.

security: (14) 1. the state of being or feeling secure; freedom from fear, anxiety, danger, doubt, etc.; state or sense of safety or certainty. —*WNWD*

sedative(s): (71) a drug that allays (calms, puts to rest) irritability, nervousness or excitement. —*WTNID*

self-determinism: (19) means the ability to direct himself.

shoal: (133) 3. shallow. —*RHCD*

231

s **shock:** (29) a person can be broken down on the emotional scale so steeply, sharply and suddenly that they can be killed. That's what's known as shock.

sinews: (20) 1. tough fibrous tissue uniting muscle to bone. —*OAD*

sing(ing) (wheel): (93) 2. to make a shrill whining or whistling sound. —*WTNID*

sinusitis: (4) inflammation of a sinus or the sinuses (3b. one of the hollow cavities in the skull connecting with the nasal cavities). —*RHCD*

sketch: (219) go over mentally. —*ed.*

slur(red): (209) 4. to speak ill of. —*OAD*

socialism: (14) an ideology which calls for state or government ownership and control of all the means of production and distribution. There is no private enterprise.

somatic: (61) body sensation, illness or pain or discomfort. *Soma* means body. Hence psychosomatic or pains stemming from the mind.

spin(ning): (6) 3. a state of mental confusion. —*AHD*

sporadic: (44) 1. happening from time to time; not constant or regular; occasional. —*WNWD*

squander(ed): (188) to spend wastefully. —*OAD*

standard: (ix) 7. a distinctive flag. —*OAD*

static(ally): (153) 3. not changing. —*OAD*

stereoscopic: (85) giving a three-dimensional effect. —*OAD*

stir(red): (172) 3. to arouse or excite or stimulate. —*OAD*

Straightwire: (63) the earliest coining of the memory exercises known as "Straightwire" came from the formula of cause and effect. We describe this as the act of stringing a line between present time and some incident in the past, and stringing that line directly and without any detours. In other words, we conceived the auditor was stringing a straight wire of memory between the actual genus [source or origin] of a condition and present time, thus demonstrating that there was a difference of time and space in the condition then and the condition now, and that the preclear conceding this difference would then rid himself of the condition or at least be able to handle it.

strip(ped): (172) 2. to deprive or dispossess (a person or thing) of (honors, titles, attributes, etc.). —*WNWD*

subjugate: (132) 1. to bring under control or subjection; conquer. —*WNWD*

sublimate: (45) 1. to divert the energy of (an emotion or impulse arising from a primitive instinct) into a culturally higher activity. —*OAD*

subversive: (15) tending or seeking to subvert (1. to overthrow or destroy something established), overthrow, or destroy an established government, institution, belief, etc.—*n.* person regarded as subversive. —*WNWD*

succumb: (13) the point marked by what one might call the death of the consciousness of the individual.

suppress(ed): (27) to squash, to sit on, to make **v** smaller, to refuse to let reach, to make uncertain about his reaching, to render or lessen in any way possible by any means possible.

susceptible: (44) easily influenced by or affected with. —*WNWD*

sustain(ed): (64) 6. to undergo or suffer (an injury, loss, etc.). —*WNWD*

sustenance: (44) 2. the food itself, nourishment. —*OAD*

swanky: (99) 1. elegant or smart. —*OAD*

symptom: (19) any circumstance, event, or condition that accompanies something and indicates its existence or occurrence; sign; indication. —*WNWD*

Tanganyika, Lake: (133) 2. a lake in central Africa between Zaïre and Tanzania: the longest fresh-water lake in the world, about 450 miles long. —*RHCD*

tenet(s): (32) a firm belief or principle or doctrine of a person or group. —*OAD*

tentative: (47) hesitant, not definite, done as a trial. —*OAD*

theta: (47) reason, serenity, stability, happiness, cheerful emotion, persistence and the other factors which man ordinarily considers desirable.

throw a wheel: (6) go into a spin or state of mental confusion. —*ed.*

thyroid: (105) a large ductless gland at the front of the neck, secreting a hormone that regulates the body's growth and development. —*OAD*

time track: (77) consists of all the consecutive moments of "now" from the earliest moment of life of the organism to present time.

toll(s): (25) 2a. to ring (a church bell, etc.) slowly with regularly repeated strokes, especially for announcing a death. —*WNWD*

tone: (5) survival potential.

tractable(-bility): (132) 1. easily managed; docile; yielding. —*RHCD*

trance: (49) 1. a half-conscious state, seemingly between sleeping and waking, in which ability to function voluntarily may be suspended.—*v.* 6. to put in a trance. —*RHCD*

tribute: (187) 1. something said or done or given as a mark of respect or admiration, etc. —*OAD*

truant officer: (6) an officer of a public school who investigates absences of pupils. —*OAD*

ulcer(s): (105) an open sore on the surface of the body or one of its organs. —*OAD*

unavailing: (34) achieving nothing, ineffectual. —*OAD*

unconsciousness: (18) a condition wherein the organism is discoordinated only in its analytical process and motor control direction.

unfounded: (108) 1. not founded on fact or truth; baseless. —*WNWD*

unsubstantial: (134) 2. without material substance. —*RHCD*

vacillate(-tion): (48) 1. to waver in decision or opinion. —*RHCD*

232

v **vacuum:** (90) 1. a space with nothing at all in it; completely empty space. —*WNWD*

vain: (114) 1. conceited, especially about one's appearance. —*OAD*

in vain: (118) with no result, uselessly. —*OAD*

validate: (133) 1. to make valid; substantiate; confirm. —*RHCD*

versus: (22) 1. in contest against. —*WNWD*

vice: (175) 1. evil or grossly immoral conduct, great wickedness. —*OAD*

vision: (18) 3. imaginative insight into a subject or problem, etc., foresight and wisdom in planning. —*OAD*

vitality: (18) 4. mental or physical vigor; energy. —*WNWD*

volatile: (45) 2. (of a person) lively, changing quickly or easily from one mood or interest to another. —*OAD*

voodoo: (31) a form of religion based on a belief in witchcraft and magical rites, practiced by some people in the West Indies and America. —*OAD*

warrant(ed): (91) 2. to serve as justification or reasonable grounds for (an act, belief, etc.). —*WNWD*

wheedle: (15) 1. to influence or persuade (a person) by flattery, soothing words, coaxing, etc. —*WNWD*

wherewithal: (14) the things (especially money) needed for a purpose. —*OAD*

wholesale: (37) 2. extensively, sweepingly or indiscriminately. —*WNWD*

wrest(ed): (185) 3. to get by effort. —*RHCD*

z **zest:** (20) 2. stimulating or exciting quality; flavor. —*WNWD*

233

234

Index

aberration; *see also* behavior
delusion and, 194
eradication of, 31
language and, 65
of emotion, 104
one of the most aberrative actions, 125
sense of touch aberrated, 100

ability, 38

A-bomb, 10, 32

abundance, 14, 151

accident prone, 26, 44

accidents, 4

action(s),
language and, 135
level of, 44
words vs., 65

"adaptive" postulate, 131

affection, 197

age,
experience and, 38
old age and reason, 18
Self Analysis and, 5
youth vs. old age, 15

agreement, 47; *see also* reality

alertness, 36

allies, 23, 152

anesthesia, 100

anger, 33, 44, 152

animals, 17

antagonism, 33, 152

anxiety, 153

apathy, 33, 44, 104, 139, 152

art, 105

arthritis, 31, 44

associations, 198

athlete, 4

atomic physics, 9

attitude, 36, 45

auditor, 6, 61, 63

awareness, 19; *see also* consciousness

bacteria, 44

behavior; *see also* aberration
fixed, 36

laws which motivate, 10
levels of, 33
momentary, 36
physiology and, 44
sexual, 45
tone scale and, 35

black and white, 85

body; *see* human body

boil-off, 71

books, 69

boredom, 34, 44

brain, 24

brain surgery, 132

bravery, 46

business, 42

calenders, 83

capabilities, 9–10

cautiousness, 37

cells, loss of, 29, 143

central nervous system, 100, 104, 119

change, 83

characteristics of people, 34

charge, 65

cheerful, 131

child, children,
anxiety toward parent, 153
attitude toward, 45
early training, 144
feeling of being small, 88
forced loss of objects, 143–44
forgetting and, 143
having to leave something alone, 144
interruptions of, 201
language and, 65, 139
punishment and, 144
slapping of, 125
suppression of, 27
tone scale and, 34

clocks, 83

clothing, 27

cold (temperature), 100

cold-blooded, 105

colds (illness), 44

collective state, 17

235

color, 68, 85

color blind, 85

communication, 47, 99, 100

communistic, 45

comparisons, 197–98

competent, mentally, 131

compliance, 207

computation(s), 37, 193, 201; see also thinking

concentration, 48

conclusions, 37

confidence, 37, 100, 132–33

confusion, 151, 195

conscious(ness); see also awareness
death of, 17
decline of, 19
definition of, 28
reduction of, 30
restoration of, 30, 32
tone scale and, 36–37
unconsciousness, 20, 30, 31, 71
what it depends upon, 31

conservatism, 37

control, 45, 207

control case, 105

conversation, 47

cooperation, 25

courage level, 46

coward, 207

cowardice, 46

criminal, 15, 28, 46, 132

criticism, 27, 49, 207

daydreaming, 193

deaf-mute, 139, 143

deafness, 91

death; see also life; pain; survival
from failures, 27
of organism, 18, 26
of reason, 18
only physical organism dies, 26
pain and, 23, 29–30, 151
passed the halfway point toward, 27
seeking death, 30
unconsciousness and, 20, 30

decision, 201

Deep Processing, 61

dejection, 104

delusion, 194

democratic, 45

depth perception, 85–86, 92

dermatitis, 31

descending spiral, 33

diabetes, 105

Dianetics, 30, 31, 38, 132

Dianetics: The Modern Science of Mental
Health, 61

diet, 31

disassociations, 198

disc,
loss of, 70
perceptions and, 66–68
use of, 59–60, 66–68

discharging unhappy incidents, 64

dishonesty, 46

distrust of motion, 125

doctor, 15

domination, 207

dreams, 15

driver, 86

dynamic principle of existence, 13

eat, refusing to, 26

education, 41

efficiency, 28

electric shock "therapy," 132

electrons, 21

elements, the, 211

emotion(s); see also tone scale
aberration of, 104
deterioration of emotional reaction, 151–52
endocrine system and, 104
experiencing of, 105
fixed emotional state about one's environment,
153
free, 105
frozen emotional reaction, 105
highest and lowest, 104
misemotionalism, 105
principal emotions, 104
recall of, 67
regulation of, 152–53
tone scale and, 44

emotionalism, 105

emotional release, 64

employing people, 42

endocrine illnesses, 44

endocrine system, 104, 105

End of Session List, 69, 219

enemies, 197–98

energy,
life is an, 21
matter and, 21
of life, 9, 131
of thought, 133

engram, 63

entheta, 47

enthusiasm, 38

entities, 151–53

environment; see also physical universe
adjusting the, 131–32
adjusting to the, 131–32
changing the, 17, 131–32
command over, 45
confusion of time and, 31
enhancing relationship with, 69
fear of, 91
fixed emotional state about, 153
low-toned, 42
man's primary foe in, 211

mastering of, 131
rehabilitating ability to know one's, 39
rehabilitating confidence in, 100
tone scale position influenced by, 41

ESP, 66

ethic level, 46

ethics, 151

euthanasia, 27, 132

exhilaration, 44

existence,
attitude toward, 36
dynamic principle of, 13

experience(s); see also incident; memory
age and, 18, 38
deintensification of unpleasant, 68
enthusiasm and, 38
hidden by pain, 36
of pleasure, 49
pain and, 19, 36–37

eye, 85–86, 195

eyesight, 100

failures, 27

fascist, 26

fascistic, 45

fear,
contrasurvival object and, 152
of environment, 91
stage fright, 201
tone scale and, 33, 44

fish, catching, 133

fluids, body, 31

food, dislike of, 100

force,
forced loss of objects, 143–44
objects forced upon one, 139
physical force, 134
use of, 133
words vs., 134

forgetting, 68, 143–44

friction, 100

friend(s),
enemies vs., 197–98
of yourself, 9, 39
trying to be like one's, 197
value as a, 50

friendship, denial of, 207

future goals, 193

glands, 105

glasses, 20

goal(s),
boredom and, 33–34
desirable goal, 23
future, 193
of life, 9
survival goal, 23
tone scale and, 33–34
your own, 9

good, man is basically, 39

good will, 28

gossip, 27, 47

grief, 33, 44, 152, 216

grogginess, 71, 119

handling of others, 49

happiness, unhappiness,
definition of, 23
discharging unhappy circumstances, 64
highest emotion is, 104
love and, 104
prosurvival entities and, 152
restoration of, 28
Self Analysis and, 5
unhappiness during Self Analysis, 69–70

health,
depends upon, 132–33
reduction of, 30
remaining healthy, 131
restoration of, 30

hearing, 91–92, 100

heart, 31 •

heat, 100

Hitlers, 28

honesty, 15, 46

hormones, 105

horse trainer, 132

Hubbard Chart of Human Evaluation, 41–53

human body; see also organism
confusion with other bodies, 195
consists of, 22
dead, 22
declining physically, 131
fluids, 31
in vs. out of the body in recall, 195
recall of position of, 67, 128
repairing itself, 31
sense of touch, 99–100

human guinea pigs, 132

hypnotic level, 49

hypothyroid conditions, 105

ideals, 14, 15, 151

ideas, 47

illness; see psychosomatic illness

imagination, 193, 194

immortality, 23, 151

impotency, 45, 100

inadequacy, 88

incident(s); see also experience; memory
earlier and earlier, 69
general, 73
grief, 216
painful, 65, 216
pleasant, 70
practice in recall of, 73
recall of 65–72
telling difference between, 91
uncomfortable as you recall, 215
unhappy, 70
unpleasant, 70

income, 14

infancy, 69

insane asylums, 28, 132

insecurity, 47

237

interest, 44

interruptions, 201

invalidation, 207–8

joint position, 128

knee, arthritis of the, 31

knife, 151

knowledge, 13, 139

language,
aberration and, 65
action and, 135
becoming more useful to you, 135
children and, 139
derivation of, 134
illusion of, 134
Niagara of, 134
symbol and, 134
trick of, 134

liberal, 45

lies, lying, 46, 47, 49

life; *see also* death; energy; survival
basic drive of, 151
begining to fail in, 131
cooperative effort, 25
energy of, 9, 131
fundamental law of, 10
fundamental purpose of, 64
goal of, 9
is an energy, 21
matter, energy, space and time vs., 64
missions of the energy of, 131
only physical organism dies, 26
pain vs. pleasure, 23
physical universe vs., 22
plotting the descending spiral of, 33
primary urge of, 22
struggle of, 151
survival and, 22
will to live, 19

life forms, 22

life potential, 32

Light Processing, 61

light waves, 85

liked vs. disliked, 50

listening, 47

lists; *see* Self Analysis lists

literalness, 48

locks, 64

loss(es), losing; *see also* pain
concentrating on, 37
enforced, 143–44
forced loss of objects, 143–44
grief and, 33
having to lose things, 143–44
of a loved one, 29
of a possession, 29
of cells, 29, 143
of survival, 29
pain and, 29, 143–44
tone scale and, 33
winning vs., 37

loudness, 67

love, 14, 15, 104

man,
actual vs. apparent worth of, 45
adjusting environment, 131–32
greatest weapon of, 17
is basically good, 39
pain's effect on, 39
reason and, 17, 18
shadows vs., 133
weather vs., 211
why he succeeds, 131–32

marital partner, 42

material universe; *see* physical universe

matter, 21

medical range, 44

medicine, 31

memory(ies); *see also* experience;
incident; recall
deintensifying of unpleasant, 70
improvement of, 3, 69, 139
misconstrued as being painful, 143–44
of pain, 36
perception of, 66

mental pain, 29

mercy killing, 27

mind,
function of, 23–24
pain and unconsciousness stored in, 30
pain knocked out of the, 38

misemotionalism, 106

mobility, 65

money, 27

monocell, 21, 22

mood, chronic, 36

motion, 68, 85, 86, 125

movies, 69

murderer, 45

music, 105

nation, 42

necessity level, 41

nervous, 91

neurological illnesses, 44

neurotic, 27

newspapers, 27

New Yorker, 38

noises, 91

nullification, 207–8

obedience, 134

object(s),
confusing one thing with another, 151
contrasurvival object, effect of, 151, 152–53
forced loss of, 144
forced upon one, 139

occlude, 143–44

occluded periods, 77

occlusion(s), 66, 77, 92

oiliness, 100

olfactory, 94–95

organic sensation, 119

organism(s); *see also* human body
becoming less competent mentally, 131
broken by force, 132
death of, 26
mobility of, 65
survival of, 23

pain; *see also* death; loss
avoiding memories of, 36–37
can be nullified or erased, 19, 20, 30, 31
death and, 23, 29, 151
definition of, 29
effect on man, 37, 39
experience and, 18–19, 36–37, 38
in processing, 71, 215, 216
knocked out of the mind, 19, 20, 38
loss and, 29, 143–44
memories misconstrued as being painful, 29, 143–44
pleasure vs., 23
sense of touch and, 100
stored in the mind, 30

painful incidents, 65

pain-storage banks, 31

pancreas, 105

parents, 153

partners, choosing, 42

people, 34

perception(s),
disc and, 59–60, 66–68
hard to contact in recall, 195
heightening of, 68
imagination and, 194
of color, 85
of memories, 66
of motion, 125
of the world, 20
orientation of senses, 83
physical universe and, 66
valence and, 195

Persian king, 10, 13

persistence, 48

personality, 195

personal motion, 67

perversion, 45

philosophy, 13

physical condition, 27

physical universe; *see also* environment
ability to handle the, 131, 132–33
choice of acceptance of the, 139
composition of, 21, 64
confidence in, 37
cutting communication with, 100
life vs., 22

physical well-being, 69, 77

physiology, 44

pictures, 85

pitch, 91

pleasure; *see also* survival
ability to experience, 49
definition of, 23
pain vs., 23
survival and, 23, 151
touch and, 100

positive suggestion, 49

possession(s), 29, 50

pressure, 100

pride, 207

prisons, 28, 132

processing section, 63–72

processing, standard, 131

procreation, 45

promiscuity, 45

protons, 21

psychosomatic ills, illness,
continually ill, 26, 44
ghosts of, 71
Self Analysis and, 4–5
stored pain and, 31
tone scale position and, 44

psychotherapy, 31

punishment, 132, 144

punishment-drive "therapies," 132

pyramid, 13

questions; *see* Self Analysis lists

rape, 45

rationality, 105

reaction time, 4

reality, 47, 133

reason, 17, 18

reasoning, 45

recall,
color vs. black and white, 85
consistently hitting physical pain and grief incidents, 216
difficulty in, 69
of incidents, 65–72
of motions, 125
of physical pain, 215
of pleasant incidents, 70
of sorrow, 216
of sound, 91–92
of unhappy incidents, 70
perceptions being hard to contact in, 195
practice in, 73
still vs. moving pictures, 85
uncomfortable as you recall incidents, 215
without depth perception, 86

recrimination, 207

rehabilitation, 30, 100

remembering, 68–69, 139, 143

resentment, 44

responsibility(ies), 28, 36, 48

restimulation, 71, 88

rheumatism, 31

rhythm, 91

Russell, Charles, 5

sadism, 45

sadness, 104

sanity, scale of, 39

science, 13

239

Science of Survival, 41, 42, 71

secondaries, 63

sedatives, 71

self, 195, 198

Self Analysis,
lists, use of, 3, 63–65
procedure, 63–72
speeds reaction time, 4
uncomfortable during, 215, 216
unhappy during, 69–70

Self Analysis lists,
end of session list, 219
going over a list many times, 70
special session lists, 215–19
use and function of, 63–72
"When Uncomfortable," 69

"self-auditing," 61

self-determinism, 134, 139, 201

self-seeking person, 26

senses, 83

sex, sexual behavior, 45, 100

shadows, 133

sight, 68, 85–86

sizes, 87–88

sleepiness, 71

small, feeling of being, 88

smell, 68, 94–95

socialism, 14

"social training," 132

society, 27

sonic, 92

sorrow, 216

sound, 67, 90–92

sound waves, 66

space, 122

special session lists, 215–19

speech, 47, 201

stage fright, 201

statements, 48

stereoscopic, 85–86, 92

Straightwire, 63

Straightwire, Repetitive, 70

striking a person, 125

subjugation, 131–32

success, 51

succumb, 13, 17

suicide, 26, 32, 45

support, 49, 207

suppression, 71

survival; *see also* death; life; pleasure
abundance and, 14, 151
basic drive of life is, 151
confusing nonsurvival and prosurvival items, 151
dynamic principle of existence is, 13
emotion and, 152
enhanced by high ideals and ethics, 151

factors, 151
fundamental purpose of life is, 64
income and, 14–15
infinity of, 23
is a graduated scale, 16
life and, 22
loss of, 29
nonsurvival, 23
of criminals, 15
of other organisms, 25
pleasure and, 151
potential, 51
seeking higher levels of, 30
society and, 27
ultimate in, 151
youth vs. old age, 15

survival potential, 42, 64–65

symbol(s), 65, 134

Tanganyika, Lake, 133

taste, 95, 100

terror, 104

Test Number One, 55

Test Number Three, 58

Test Number Two, 57

thing; *see* object

thinking, 193, 201; *see also* computation

thinking abilities, 69

thought(s), 133, 144

threat(s), 49, 152–53

thyroid, 105

time,
aiding sense of, 77, 83
confusion of environment and, 31
telling difference between one time and another, 91

time orientation, 77

time track, 77

today, 37

tone (sound), 68, 91

tone, tone level, 5, 41–42

tone scale; *see also* emotion
behavior and, 35
being at high level of, 36, 39
chronic or acute aspects of, 35, 36, 41
consciousness and, 36–37
derivation of, 144
diagram of, 44–51
education and one's position on the, 41
emotions and, 104
environment influences one's position on the, 41–42
finding oneself on the, 35–36, 55
going up or down on the, 35, 36–37, 152
pain causing decline on the, 36–37
what it does, 34

touch, 68, 99–100

truth, 46

ulcers, 105

uncomfortable, 69

unconsciousness; *see* consciousness

understood, 51

240

unhappiness; *see* happiness

vacuum, 90–91
valences, 195, 197
viewpoint, 195
vitality, 30
volume, 91
voodoo, 31

war, 28
weather, 211
weight, 67
welfare state, 131–32
"When Uncomfortable," 69
will to live, 19

win, 37
words, 65, 134
world, 19, 20, 28
worth, 45

yawning, 71, 119
yesterday, 37
youth, 15, 18

241

242

Bibliography

Basic Dianetics Books

You've read *Self Analysis*. Now get the rest of the Basic Dianetics Books Package—your complete guide to the inner workings of the mind. You can get all of these books individually or in a set, complete with an attractive slipcase.

Dianetics: The Modern Science of Mental Health • Acclaimed as the most effective self-help book ever published. Dianetics technology has helped millions reach new heights of freedom and ability. Millions of copies are sold every year! Discover the source of mental barriers that prevent you from achieving your goals—and how to handle them!

The Dynamics of Life • Break through the barriers to your happiness. This is the first book Ron wrote detailing the startling principles behind Dianetics—facts so powerful they can change forever the way you look at yourself and your potentials. Discover how you can use the powerful basic principles in this book to blast through the barriers of your mind and gain full control over your success, future and happiness.

Dianetics: The Evolution of a Science • It is estimated that we use less than ten percent of our mind's potential. What stops us from developing and using the full potential of our minds? *Dianetics: The Evolution of a Science* is L. Ron Hubbard's incredible story of how he discovered the reactive mind and how he developed the keys to unlock its secrets. Get this firsthand account of what the mind really is, and how you can release its hidden potential.

Dianetics Graduate Books

These books by L. Ron Hubbard give you detailed knowledge of how the mind works—data you can use to help yourself and others break out of the traps of life. While you can get these books individually, the Dianetics Graduate Books Package can also be purchased as a set, complete with an attractive slipcase.

Science of Survival • If you ever wondered why people act the way they do, you'll find this book a wealth of information. It's vital to anyone who wants to understand others and improve personal relationships. *Science of Survival* is built around a remarkable chart—The Hubbard Chart of Human Evaluation. With it you can understand and predict other people's behavior and reactions and greatly increase your control over your own life. This is a valuable handbook that can make a difference between success and failure on the job and in life.

Dianetics 55! • Your success in life depends on your ability to communicate. Do you know a formula exists for communication? Learn the rules of better communication that can help you live a more fulfilling life. Here, L. Ron Hubbard deals with the fundamental principles of communication and how you can master these to achieve your goals.

Advanced Procedure and Axioms • For the *first* time the basics of thought and the physical universe have been codified into a set of fundamental laws, signaling an entirely new way to view and approach the subjects of man, the physical universe and even life itself.

Handbook for Preclears • Written as an advanced personal workbook, *Handbook for Preclears* contains easily done processes to help you overcome the effect of times you were not in control of your life, times that your emotions were a barrier to your success and much more. Completing all the fifteen auditing steps contained in this book sets you up for really being in *control* of your environment and life.

Child Dianetics • Here is a revolutionary new approach to rearing children with Dianetics auditing techniques. Find out how you can help your child achieve greater confidence, more self-reliance, improved learning rate and a happier, more loving relationship with you.

Notes on the Lectures of L. Ron Hubbard • Compiled from his fascinating lectures given shortly after the publication of *Dianetics*, this book contains some of the first material Ron ever released on the ARC triangle and the Tone Scale, and how these discoveries relate to auditing.

Learn how to USE Dianetics technology at a hands-on *Dianetics Seminar*

We were all born with a mental computer far more sophisticated than the most advanced computers in the world today. However, we are not trained in how to USE this incredible computer to solve our problems and worries and unblock our full natural capacity.

Now in just one weekend (or five evenings), you can get practical hands-on experience in handling this amazing computer and using Dianetics technology to better your life. The *Hubbard Dianetics Seminar* is designed to give you an introduction to Dianetics principles and techniques, on an easy, enjoyable gradient.

People who have done the *Hubbard Dianetics Seminar* have reported:

- Return of enthusiasm for life
- Increased self-confidence
- The ability to instantly help someone else

  —and much more!

Don't put up with the stresses, worries and upsets in life any longer. Start on the road to a happier life with the *Hubbard Dianetics Seminar.*

Start today!

Contact the Public Registrar at your nearest Hubbard Dianetics Foundation.

(A complete list of Hubbard Dianetics Foundations is provided at the back of this book.)

Begin a better life with Dianetics Extension Courses

Dianetics books by L. Ron Hubbard provide the knowledge needed to understand and use the world's most incredible computer—your own mind. Now learn to *use* that knowledge to gain greater happiness and self-confidence in life. Enroll on a Dianetics Extension Course.

Each extension course package includes a lesson booklet with easy-to-understand instructions and all the lessons you will need to complete it. Each course can be done in the comfort of your own home or right in your local Hubbard Dianetics Foundation. Your Extension Course Supervisor will review each lesson as you complete it (or mail it in if you do the course at home) and get the results right back to you. When you complete the course you get a beautiful certificate, suitable for framing.

The Dynamics of Life
Extension Course

Based on L. Ron Hubbard's concise introduction to the subject of Dianetics. This course takes you through L. Ron Hubbard's first book on the subject and helps to teach you the basics of the mind and how it *really* works. Order your copy today!

Self Analysis
Extension Course

How good can you get? How much can you improve your life? The *Self Analysis Extension Course* takes you through the book *Self Analysis* and helps you get a full understanding and ability to apply the materials in it. *Self Analysis* is a complete do-it-yourself manual for personal improvement, and this home study course will get you the maximum benefits from the exercises contained in this book. Order your copy today!

The Dianetics
Extension Course

Based on the book *Dianetics: The Modern Science of Mental Health,* this course takes you step-by-step through the book, helping you to understand each part as you go along. The lessons pinpoint key data in the book. You'll learn about Clear, the reactive mind, the analytical mind and the complete technology of Dianetics. Order your copy today!

Dianetics: The Evolution of a Science
Extension Course

Based on L. Ron Hubbard's introduction to Dianetics, this course will help you gain a basic understanding of the principles and techniques of Dianetics. You'll also get a better understanding of how L. Ron Hubbard discovered the principles of Dianetics, and how he developed the techniques that are used today around the world to create happier, more successful lives. Order your copy today!

Enroll on a Dianetics
Extension Course Today!

For information and enrollment and prices for these Extension Courses and the books they accompany, contact the Public Registrar at your nearest Hubbard Dianetics Foundation. (A complete list of Hubbard Dianetics Foundations is provided at the back of this book.)

Get Your Free Catalog of Knowledge on How to Improve Life

L. Ron Hubbard's books and tapes increase your ability to understand yourself and others. His works give you the practical know-how you need to improve your life and the lives of your family and friends.

Many more materials by L. Ron Hubbard are available than have been covered in the pages of this book. A free catalog of these materials is available on request.

Write for your free catalog today!

NEW ERA Publications International ApS
Store Kongensgade 53
1264 Copenhagen K, Denmark

Continental Publications Pty Ltd.
PO Box 27080, Benrose
Johannesburg 2011
Republic of South Africa

NEW ERA Publications United Kingdom Ltd.
Saint Hill Manor
East Grinstead, West Sussex
England RH19 4JY

NEW ERA Publications Australia Pty Ltd.
61–65 Wentworth Avenue, Level 1
Surry Hills, New South Wales
2010, Australia

"I am always happy to hear from my readers."

L. Ron Hubbard

These were the words of L. Ron Hubbard, who was always very interested in hearing from his friends and readers. He made a point of staying in communication with everyone he came in contact with over his fifty-year career as a professional writer, and he had thousands of fans and friends that he corresponded with all over the world.

The publishers of L. Ron Hubbard's works wish to continue this tradition and welcome letters and comments from you, his readers, both old and new.

Additionally, the publishers will be happy to send you information on anything you would like to know about Ron, his extraordinary life and accomplishments and the vast number of books he has written.

Any message addressed to the Author's Affairs Director at NEW ERA Publications will be given prompt and full attention.

NEW ERA Publications International ApS
Store Kongensgade 53
1264 Copenhagen K, Denmark

Address List

The Hubbard Dianetics Foundation is a department within the Church of Scientology and every Church of Scientology has a Hubbard Dianetics Foundation.

If you would like more information about Dianetics auditing, lectures, workshops or seminars, contact your nearest organization today.

USA

Albuquerque

Church of Scientology
8106 Menaul Blvd. N.E.
Albuquerque, New Mexico 87110

Ann Arbor

Church of Scientology
2355 West Stadium Blvd.
Ann Arbor, Michigan 48103

Atlanta

Church of Scientology
1611 Mt. Vernon Road
Dunwoody, Georgia 30338

Austin

Church of Scientology
2200 Guadalupe
Austin, Texas 78705

Boston

Church of Scientology
448 Beacon Street
Boston, Massachusetts 02115

Buffalo

Church of Scientology
47 West Huron Street
Buffalo, New York 14202

Chicago

Church of Scientology
3011 North Lincoln Avenue
Chicago, Illinois 60657-4207

Cincinnati

Church of Scientology
215 West 4th Street, 5th Floor
Cincinnati, Ohio 45202-2670

Clearwater

Church of Scientology
Flag Service Organization
210 South Fort Harrison Avenue
Clearwater, Florida 33756

Church of Scientology
Flag Ship Service Organization
c/o *Freewinds* Relay Office
118 N. Fort Harrison Avenue
Clearwater, Florida 33755

Columbus

Church of Scientology
30 North High Street
Columbus, Ohio 43215

Dallas

Church of Scientology
Celebrity Centre Dallas
10500 Steppington Drive,
    Suite 100
Dallas, Texas 75230

Denver

Church of Scientology
3385 S. Bannock
Englewood, Colorado 80110

Detroit

Church of Scientology
321 Williams Street
Royal Oak, Michigan 48067

Honolulu

Church of Scientology
1148 Bethel Street
Honolulu, Hawaii 96813

Kansas City

Church of Scientology
3619 Broadway
Kansas City, Missouri 64111

Las Vegas
Church of Scientology
846 East Sahara Avenue
Las Vegas, Nevada 89104

Church of Scientology
Celebrity Centre Las Vegas
1100 South 10th Street
Las Vegas, Nevada 89104

Long Island
Church of Scientology
99 Railroad Station Plaza
Hicksville, New York 11801

Los Angeles and vicinity
Church of Scientology
4810 Sunset Boulevard
Los Angeles, California 90027

Church of Scientology
1451 Irvine Boulevard
Tustin, California 92680

Church of Scientology
1277 East Colorado Boulevard
Pasadena, California 91106

Church of Scientology
15643 Sherman Way
Van Nuys, California 91406

Church of Scientology
American Saint Hill Organization
1413 L. Ron Hubbard Way
Los Angeles, California 90027

Church of Scientology
American Saint Hill Foundation
1413 L. Ron Hubbard Way
Los Angeles, California 90027

Church of Scientology
Advanced Organization of
   Los Angeles
1306 L. Ron Hubbard Way
Los Angeles, California 90027

Church of Scientology
Celebrity Centre International
5930 Franklin Avenue
Hollywood, California 90028

Los Gatos
Church of Scientology
2155 S. Bascom Avenue
Campbell, California 95008

Miami
Church of Scientology
120 Giralda Avenue
Coral Gables, Florida 33134

Minneapolis
Church of Scientology
Twin Cities
1011 Nicollet Mall
Minneapolis, Minnesota 55403

Mountain View
Church of Scientology
2483 Old Middlefield Way
Mountain View, California 96043

Nashville
Church of Scientology
Celebrity Centre Nashville
2483 Old Murfreesboro Pike
Nashville, Tennessee 37212

New Haven
Church of Scientology
909 Whalley Avenue
New Haven
Connecticut 06515-1728

New York City
Church of Scientology
227 West 46th Street
New York City
New York 10036-1409

Church of Scientology
Celebrity Centre New York
65 East 82nd Street
New York City, New York 10028

Orlando
Church of Scientology
1830 East Colonial Drive
Orlando, Florida 32803-4729

Philadelphia
Church of Scientology
1315 Race Street
Philadelphia, Pennsylvania 19107

Phoenix
Church of Scientology
2111 W. University Dr.
Mesa, Arizona 85201

Portland
Church of Scientology
2636 N.E. Sandy Boulevard
Portland, Oregon 97232-2342

Church of Scientology
Celebrity Centre Portland
708 S.W. Salmon Street
Portland, Oregon 97205

Sacramento
Church of Scientology
825 15th Street
Sacramento
California 95814-2096

Salt Lake City
Church of Scientology
1931 S. 1100 East
Salt Lake City, Utah 84106

San Diego
Church of Scientology
1330 4th Ave.
San Diego, California 92101

San Francisco
Church of Scientology
83 McAllister Street
San Francisco, California 94102

San Jose
Church of Scientology
80 E. Rosemary
San Jose, California 95112

Santa Barbara
Church of Scientology
524 State Street
Santa Barbara, California 93101

Seattle
Church of Scientology
2226 3rd Avenue
Seattle, Washington 98121

St. Louis
Church of Scientology
6901 Delmar Boulevard
University City, Missouri 63130

Tampa
Church of Scientology
3617 Henderson Blvd.
Tampa, Florida 33609-4501

Washington, DC
Founding Church of Scientology
of Washington, DC
1701 20th Street N.W.
Washington, DC 20009

Puerto Rico

Hato Rey
Church of Scientology
272 JT Piñero Avenue
Hyde Park, Hato Rey
Puerto Rico 00918

Canada

Edmonton
Church of Scientology
10206 106th Steet N.W.
Edmonton, Alberta
Canada T5J 1H7

Kitchener
Church of Scientology
104 King St. West, 2nd Floor
Kitchener, Ontario
Canada N2G 1A6

Montreal
Church of Scientology
4489 Papineau Street
Montréal, Québec
Canada H2H 1T7

Ottawa
Church of Scientology
150 Rideau Street, 2nd Floor
Ottawa, Ontario
Canada K1N 5X6

Quebec
Church of Scientology
350 Bd Chareste Est
Québec, Québec
Canada G1K 3H5

Toronto
Church of Scientology
696 Yonge Street, 2nd Floor
Toronto, Ontario
Canada M4Y 2A7

Vancouver
Church of Scientology
401 West Hasting Street
Vancouver, British Columbia
Canada V6B 1L5

Winnipeg
Church of Scientology
315 Garry Street, Suite 210
Winnipeg, Manitoba
Canada R3B 2G7

United Kingdom

Birmingham
Church of Scientology
8 Ethel Street
Winston Churchill House
Birmingham, England B2 4BG

Brighton
Church of Scientology
Third Floor
79-83 North Street
Brighton, Sussex
England BN1 1ZA

East Grinstead
Church of Scientology
Saint Hill Foundation
Saint Hill Manor
East Grinstead, West Sussex
England RH19 4JY

Advanced Organization
Saint Hill
Saint Hill Manor
East Grinstead, West Sussex
England RH19 4JY

Edinburgh

Hubbard Academy of
    Personal Independence
20 Southbridge
Edinburgh, Scotland EH1 1LL

London

Church of Scientology
68 Tottenham Court Road
London, England W1P 0BB

Manchester

Church of Scientology
258 Deansgate
Manchester, England M3 4BG

Plymouth

Church of Scientology
41 Ebrington Street
Plymouth, Devon

England PL4 9AA

Sunderland

Church of Scientology
51 Fawcett Street
Sunderland, Tyne and Wear
England SR1 1RS

Austria

Vienna

Church of Scientology
Schottenfeldgasse 13/15
1070 Wien, Austria

Church of Scientology
Celebrity Centre Vienna
Senefeldergasse 11/5
1100 Wien, Austria

Belgium

Brussels

Church of Scientology
61, General MacArthur
1180 Bruxelles, Belgium

Denmark

Aarhus

Church of Scientology
Vester Alle 26
8000 Aarhus C, Denmark

Copenhagen

Church of Scientology
Store Kongensgade 55
1264 Copenhagen K, Denmark

Church of Scientology
Gammel Kongevej 3–5, 1
1610 Copenhagen V, Denmark

Church of Scientology
Advanced Organization
    Saint Hill for Europe and Africa
Jernbanegade 6
1608 Copenhagen V, Denmark

France

Angers

Church of Scientology
28B, avenue Mendès
49240 Avrille, France

Clermont-Ferrand

Church of Scientology
6, rue Dulaure
63000 Clermont-Ferrand, France

Lyon

Church of Scientology
3, place des Capucins
69001 Lyon, France

Paris

Church of Scientology
7, rue Jules César
75012 Paris, France

Church of Scientology
Celebrity Centre Paris
69, rue Legendre
75017 Paris, France

Saint-Étienne

Church of Scientology
24, rue Marengo
42000 Saint-Étienne, France

Germany

Berlin

Church of Scientology
Sponholzstraße 51–52
12159 Berlin, Germany

Düsseldorf

Church of Scientology
Friedrichstraße 28
40217 Düsseldorf, Germany

Church of Scientology
Celebrity Centre Düsseldorf
Luisenstraße 23
40215 Düsseldorf, Germany

Frankfurt

Church of Scientology
Kaiserstraße 49
60329 Frankfurt, Germany

Hamburg

Church of Scientology
Domstraße 9
20095 Hamburg, Germany

Church of Scientology
Brennerstraße 12
20099 Hamburg, Germany

Hannover
Church of Scientology
Odeonstraße 17
30159 Hannover, Germany

Munich
Church of Scientology
Beichstraße 12
80802 Munich, Germany

Church of Scientology
Celebrity Centre Munich
Landshuter Allee 42
80637 Munich, Germany

Stuttgart
Church of Scientology
Hohenheimerstr. 9
70184 Stuttgart, Germany

Israel
Tel Aviv
College of Dianetics and
    Scientology
12 Shontzino Street
PO Box 57478
61573 Tel Aviv, Israel

Italy
Brescia
Church of Scientology
Via Fratelli Bronzetti, 20
25122 Brescia, Italy

Catania
Church of Scientology
Via Garibaldi, 9
95121 Catania, Italy

Florence
Church of Scientology
Celebrity Centre Florence
Via Silvestrina, 12, 1st floor
50129 Florence, Italy

Milan
Church of Scientology
Via Lepontina, 4
20159 Milano, Italy

Monza
Church of Scientology
Via Largo Molinetto, 1
20052 Monza (MI), Italy

Novara
Church of Scientology
Corso Milano, 28
28100 Novara, Italy

Nuoro
Church of Scientology
Via Lamarmora, 102
08100 Nuoro, Italy

Padua
Church of Scientology
Via Ugo Foscolo, 5
35131 Padova, Italy

Pordenone
Church of Scientology
Via Dogana, 19
Zona Fiera
33170 Pordenone, Italy

Rome
Church of Scientology
Via del Caravita, 5
00186 Rome, Italy

Turin
Church of Scientology
Via Bersezio, 7
10152 Torino, Italy

Verona
Church of Scientology
Corso Milano, 84
37138 Verona, Italy

Netherlands
Amsterdam
Church of Scientology
Nieuwezijds Voorburgwal 116-118
1012 SH Amsterdam, Netherlands

Norway
Oslo
Church of Scientology
Storgata 17
0184 Oslo, Norway

Portugal
Lisbon
Church of Scientology
Rua da Prata 185,2
1100 Lisbon, Portugal

Russia
Moscow
Hubbard Humanitarian Center
Ul. Borisa Galushkina 19A
129301 Moscow, Russia

Spain
Barcelona
Dianetics Civil Association
Pasaje Domingo, 11-13 Bajos
08007 Barcelona, Spain

Madrid
Dianetics Civil Association
Villa Maria
C/ Montera 20, Piso 1º dcha.
28013 Madrid, Spain

Sweden
Göteborg
Church of Scientology
Wärmlandsgatan 16, 1 tr.
413 28 Göteborg, Sweden

Malmö
Church of Scientology
Porslingsgatan 3
211 32 Malmö, Sweden

Stockholm
Church of Scientology
Götgatan 105
116 62 Stockholm, Sweden

Switzerland
Basel
Church of Scientology
Herrengrabenweg 56
4054 Basel, Switzerland

Bern
Church of Scientology
Muhlemattstr. 31, Postfach 384
3000 Bern 14, Switzerland

Geneva
Church of Scientology
12, rue des Acacias
1227 Carouge
Genève, Switzerland

Lausanne
Church of Scientology
10, rue de la Madeleine
1003 Lausanne, Switzerland

Zurich
Church of Scientology
Freilagerstrasse 11
8047 Zürich, Switzerland

Australia
Adelaide
Church of Scientology
24–28 Waymouth Street
Adelaide, South Australia 5000
Australia

Brisbane
Church of Scientology
106 Edward Street, 2nd Floor
Brisbane, Queensland 4000
Australia

Canberra
Church of Scientology
43–45 East Row
Canberra City, ACT 2601
Australia

Melbourne
Church of Scientology
42–44 Russell Street
Melbourne, Victoria 3000
Australia

Perth
Church of Scientology
108 Murray Street, 1st Floor
Perth, Western Australia 6000
Australia

Sydney
Church of Scientology
201 Castlereagh Street
Sydney, New South Wales 2000
Australia

Church of Scientology
Advanced Organization Saint Hill
　Australia, New Zealand and
　Oceania
19–37 Greek Street
Glebe, New South Wales 2037
Australia

Japan
Tokyo
Scientology Tokyo
2-11-7 Kita-Otsuka
Toshima-Ku
Tokyo, Japan 170-0004

New Zealand
Auckland
Church of Scientology
159 Queen Street, 3rd Floor
Auckland 1, New Zealand

Africa
Bulawayo
Church of Scientology
Southampton House, Suite 202
Main Street and 9th Ave.
Bulawayo, Zimbabwe

Cape Town
Church of Scientology
Ground Floor, Dorlane House
39 Roeland Street
Cape Town 8001
Republic of South Africa

Durban

Church of Scientology
20 Buckinham Terrace
Westville, 3630 Durban
South Africa

Harare

Church of Scientology
404-409 Pockets Building
50 Jason Moyo Avenue
Harare, Zimbabwe

Johannesburg

Church of Scientology
4th Floor, Budget House
130 Main Street
Johannesburg 2001
South Africa

Church of Scientology
No. 108, 1st Floor,
    Bordeaux Centre
Gordon Road, Corner
    Jan Smuts Avenue
Blairgowrie, Randburg 2125
South Africa

Port Elizabeth

Church of Scientology
2 St. Christopher's
27 Westbourne Road Central
Port Elizabeth 6001
South Africa

Pretoria

Church of Scientology
307 Ancore Building
Corner Jeppe and Esselen Streets
Sunnyside, Pretoria 0002
South Africa

Argentina

Buenos Aires

Dianetics Association of
    Argentina
2162 Batolomé Mitre
Buenos Aires 1039, Argentina

Colombia

Bogotá

Dianetics Cultural Center
Carrera 30 #91–96
Bogotá, Colombia

Mexico

Guadalajara

Dianetics Cultural
    Organization, A.C.
Ave. de la Paz 2787
Fracc. Arcos Sur
Sector Juárez,
    Guadalajara, Jalisco
C.P. 44500, México

Mexico City

Dianetics Cultural
    Association, A.C.
Belisario Domínguez #17-1
Coyoacán, Centro
C.P. 04000, México, D.F.

Dianetics Cultural
    Organization, A.C.
Calle Monterrey #402
Colonia Narvarte
C.P. 03020, México, D.F.

Dianetics Development
    Organization, A.C.
Xola #1113, Esq. Pitágoras
Colonia Narvarte
C.P. 03220, México, D.F.

Dianetics Technological
    Institute, A.C.
Avenida Chapultepec #40
Colonia Roma
C.P. 11590, México, D.F.

Institute of Applied Philosophy
    Center, A.C.
Isabel la Católica #24
Centro Histórico de la Ciudad
    de Mexico
C.P. 06890, México, D.F.

Latin American Cultural
    Center, A.C.
Rio Amazonas 11
Colonia Cuauhtemoc
C.P. 06500, México, D.F.

Venezuela

Caracas

Dianetics Cultural
    Organization, A.C.
Avenida Principal de las Palmas,
    Cruce Con Calle Carúpano
Quinta Suha, Las Palmas
Caracas, Venezuela

Valencia

Dianetics Cultural
    Association, A.C.
Avenida 101, 150-23
Urbanización La Alegría
Apartado Postal 833
Valencia, Venezuela

To obtain any books by L. Ron Hubbard which are not available at your local organization, contact any of the following publishers:

NEW ERA Publications
International ApS
Store Kongensgade 53
1264 Copenhagen K, Denmark

Continental Publications
Pty Ltd.
PO Box 27080, Benrose
Johannesburg 2011
Republic of South Africa

NEW ERA Publications
UK, Ltd.
Saint Hill Manor
East Grinstead, West Sussex
England RH19 4JY

NEW ERA Publications
Australia Pty Ltd.
61–65 Wentworth Avenue, Level 1
Surry Hills, New South Wales
2010, Australia

NEW ERA Publications Italia Srl
Via Cadorna, 61
20090 Vimodrone (MI), Italy

NEW ERA Publications
Deutschland GmbH
Hittfelder Kirchweg 5a
21220 Seevetal-Machen
Germany

NEW ERA Publications
France E.U.R.L.
14, rue des Moulins
75001 Paris, France

Representante de
NEW ERA Publications
C/ Miguel Menendez Boneta 18
28460 Los Molinos, Madrid, Spain

NEW ERA Publications Japan, Inc.
4-38-15-2F Higashi Ikebukuro
Toshima-Ku
Tokyo, Japan 108

NEW ERA Publications Group
Str. Kasatkina, 16, Building 1
129301 Moscow, Russia

Bridge Publications, Inc.
4751 Fountain Avenue
Los Angeles
California 90029

Rua Alfonso Celso 115
Vila Mariana São Paulo, SP
04119-000 Brazil

Continental Publications
Liaison Office
696 Yonge Street
Toronto, Ontario
Canada M4Y 2A7

ERA DINÁMICA EDITORES,
S.A. de C.V.
Pablo Ucello #16
Colonia C.D. de los Deportes
Mexico, D.F.

To obtain any cassettes by L. Ron Hubbard which are not available at your local organization, contact:

Golden Era Productions
6331 Hollywood Boulevard, Suite 1305
Los Angeles, California 90028-6313, USA